D0198704

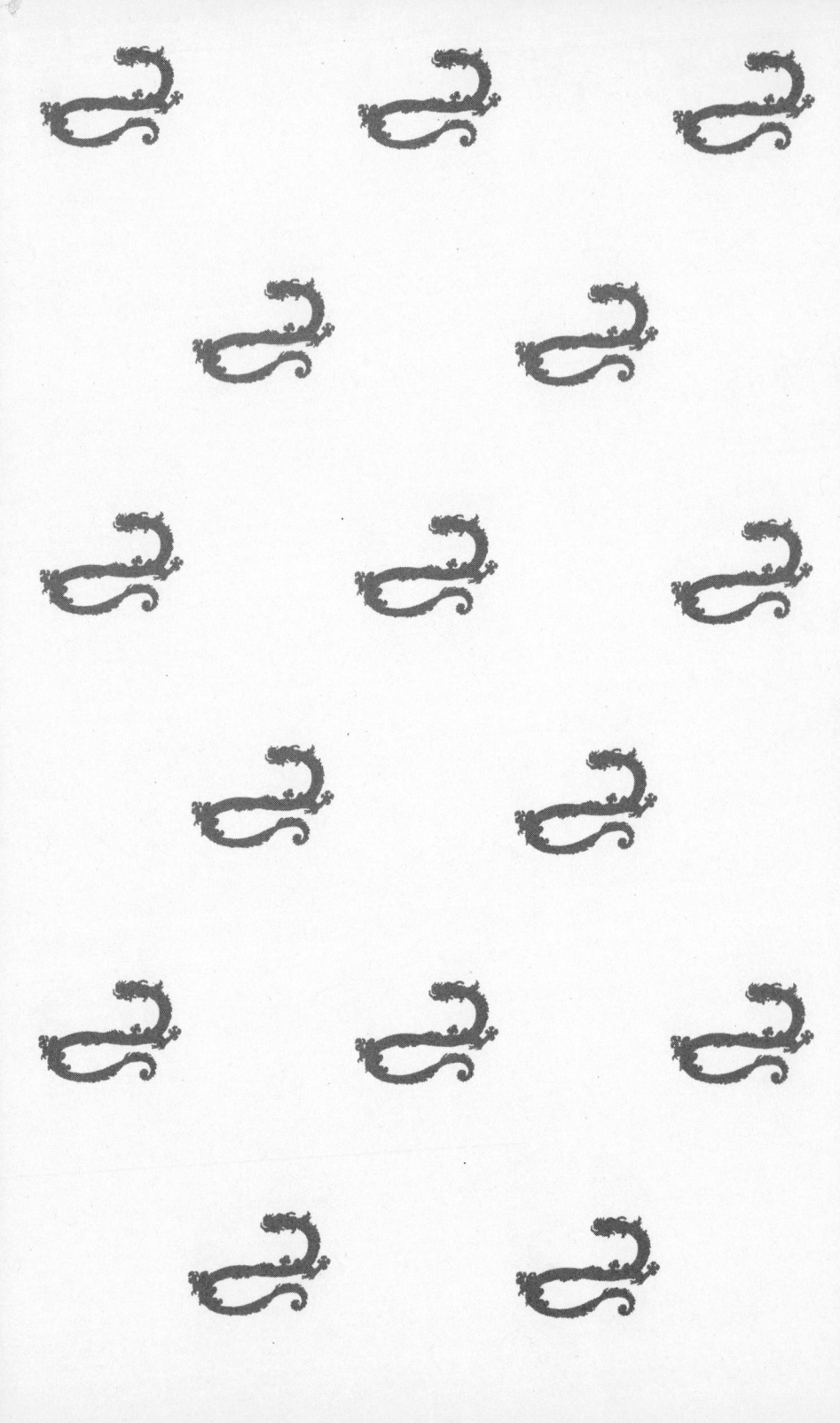

THE JADE EMPEROR'S MIND SEAL CLASSIC
—A Taoist Guide to Health, Longevity and Immortality—

The Jade Emperor's
MIND SEAL CLASSIC

—A Taoist Guide to Health, Longevity and Immortality—

Translation and Commentary by Stuart Alve Olson

Dragon
Door

Dragon Door Publications
P.O. Box 4381
St. Paul, MN 55104, USA

First Edition, February 1993
Second Printing, May 1993

Library of Congress Catalog Card Number: 92-73714
ISBN 0-938045-10-5

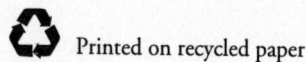 Printed on recycled paper

Dedicated to the memory of Liang Shu-wen

Acknowledgements

Much appreciation goes to Master T.T. Liang for first giving me his copy of the Jade Emperor's Mind Seal Classic, for helping me initially with some of the more difficult concepts expressed in the work and for his contribution of the cover calligraphy. But mostly I wish to thank him for his years of instruction, guidance and friendship, which has made life itself more enjoyable. He is truly a living immortal.

To Professor Wu Yi, who first taught me about Lao Tzu's thought during my residency at the City of Ten-Thousands Buddhas, my deepest gratitude for all his patient tutoring.

Without question I must thank all the monks at the City of Ten-Thousand Buddhas. They changed the course of my life and by pure example revealed to me the meaning of self-cultivation. To them I bow in deep respect.

To my wife, Loa Lian-hwa, for patiently typing out the first draft of this work and for her constant insistence that I finish this project before daring to enter my files of numerous other unfinished materials. To her I yield and say thank you.

To John Du Cane, who again through his editing allows me to say what I mean, so that I may mean what I say. No easy task.

Again, many thanks to the "book wizard" Randy Scholes for his book and cover design and to Mike Urseth for getting it all into and out of the computer the way it is supposed to be.

To The Minneapolis Institute of Art and The John R. Van Derlip Fund for permission to use the photographs for the cover art and frontispiece.

Finally, I wish to acknowledge the indispensable help given so generously during the many phases of this book by Jay and Page Cowles, Joanne Von Blon, Harry Cunliffe, Richard Peterson, Larry Hawkins, Lara Puffer, Fred Marych and, possibly, by the Jade Emperor himself.

THE JADE EMPEROR'S MIND SEAL CLASSIC

The Jade Emperor seated in his court passing judgements.

Introduction

To my knowledge this is the first English translation of this popular Taoist text. Admittedly, when I first read through the text, I was not all that enthusiastic about translating it. It appeared to be no more than a jumbled collection of Taoist aphorisms, disjointed and unclear in purpose. For one reason or another I kept finding myself returning to it as a reference while working on other Taoist works. Eventually I realized why Taoist monks, especially of the *Chuan Chen* (Complete Reality) and *Lung Men* (Dragon Door) sects of the White Cloud Monastery, in Beijing, found it so valuable in their daily rituals and festival ceremonies. The text is, without question, a very concise overview of what each Taoist aspires to spiritually.

Hopefully, as readers, you will come to share my belief in the importance of this text. I have, with limited knowledge, attempted to make clear the entire text, from the title to the passages. The real difficulty in doing this however is that the verses of the text are in the framework of mystical experience. The language of the mystic is very difficult to adapt into everyday language, for the very nature of mystical experience is beyond normal mundane experiences and language. Therefore, in order to further clarify the text I have added a work from the Lung Men sect, *The Three Treasures of Immortality*, a discourse with various verses from accomplished *tao shih* (Taoist masters) of the past, which reveals a great deal about Taoist thought, especially in connection with this text.

The Chinese Phonetic Text, for Recitation has also been

provided. The original use of this text was for recitation. I
felt obliged to make this aspect of it available.

Lastly I've included a *Translator's Afterword*, which is a
brief account of my experience with meditation and a sum-
mary of both the obstacles and impasses of practice.

The underlying message of this classic is that within
each of us dwells the medicine to cure the affliction of mortality. We possess the seeds of primal forces, which if cultivated properly will confer great spiritual benefits. The "open
secret" of nourishing these seeds is none other than our own
tranquility - to let the dust settle so that we may see with
utmost clarity these seeds of immortality.

This text is extremely important to our modern day
society, if not for the achievement of immortality, a most difficult concept for many Westerners, then certainly for the
achievement of health, longevity and spiritual insight. With
all the stresses and illnesses afflicting our society, the experience of tranquility within ourselves could be the greatest
medicine of all. We need not accept the lofty Taoist goal of
immortality to understand and seek out these other jewels
along the way.

For those not deeply familiar with Taoist thought it is
essential to understand that it is not religious, in the Judeo-
Christian sense of the word. Both in its philosophical origins
and in its form as an organized religious system, Taoism is
devoid of dogmatism. The *I Ching* (Book of Changes) says,
"All things on earth are first an archetype in heaven."
Taoism is an expression of this statement, adopting the ways
of heaven as an example for living on this earth. Gods, to the
daily life of Taoists, have about as much importance as kan-
garoos do to people living in New York. They accept their
existence, but not their relevancy. To the Taoist, Gods are
mythical symbols, engaged in to draw out the spiritual, heav-

enly like qualities within us. Taoism sees no conflict in maintaining an outer shell that has a religious appearance, while holding to the inner belief that all things are returnable to the source, Tao.

In conclusion, I hope this work provides something of use to the reader. This work is mostly due to my fortunate fate of having studied and met with men who justly deserve the title of "immortal". At best I serve as a tiny mirror reflecting just a bit of their vast wisdom light.

Translator
Autumn, 1992

Historical Background

This brief text was probably composed sometime during the Sung dynasty, under the reign of Emperor Hui Tsung, who had originally deified the Jade Emperor as Lord On High and erected temples in his honor. There are two extant texts of this classic, and other various texts which use the term *Mind Seal* within the titles. But it is two texts, one arranged by Lu Szu-hsing and a later version by Chio Chen Tzu, which prove the most valuable. Both have commentaries attached to them. The earlier of the two is the Ming dynasty text, titled, *Yu Huang Hsin Yin Miao Ching* (The Jade Emperor's Profound Mind-Seal Classic), which has a commentary by Lu Szu-hsing.

Lu Szu-hsing states in his commentary that the most important verse of the entire text is, *keep to non-being, yet hold onto being,* which is taken directly from the *Tao Te Ching* (Classic on the Way and Virtue). An adept's empirical understanding of the meaning in this verse will help him reverse the light of the *yuan shen* (primal spirit). This in turn will create a "quickening of the ch'i" and enable the achievement of self-illumination. The verse points directly to the experience of creating a spiritual embryo - a being, yet non-being. More on this later.

Within Lu Szu-hsing's version of this classic are appended verses which do not appear in other compilations, suggesting that they are most likely his own inventions. Chio Chen Tzu, of the Ching dynasty, omitted these verses in his re-formation of the text, which is presently the accepted version of the classic. For sake of clarity I have placed Lu's appended verses at the end of the English translation, thus restoring his original twenty-four sections.

Lu Szu-hsing divided the text into twenty-four separate verses (Chio Chen Tzu discarded this arrangement), and provided select discourses on nourishing the ching and ch'i, inner alchemy, congealing the elixir and releasing the spirit embryo. In his introduction to the text he provides many related quotations from not only Taoist, but Buddhist and Confucianist sources. The entire work is presented in much the same manner as *The Secret of the Golden Flower* (T'ai I Chin Hua Tsung Chih), while retaining a greater sense and flavor of Taoism and being much less eclectic. It can also be a bit confusing to the non-initiate. Chio Chen Tzu did well to simplify the text and commentary. The work presented here lies somewhere in the middle of these two, while leaning towards the Chio Chen Tzu version.

There is no clear evidence as to who the original author of this text truly is. On the one hand this is really not so important. On the other hand the terminology used throughout the text is quite important, as many of the ideas are derived either directly from the *Tao Te Ching*, or from the *Chuang Tzu* and *Pao P'o Tzu*.

To determine the period of original authorship would help clarify whether or not the cult of the Jade Emperor was an integral part of early folk religion, portions of which Taoism adapted to its beliefs, or whether it was an invention of the first organizer of popular Taoist religion, Chang Tao-ling (born 34 A.D., Later Han dynasty. He is considered to have lived 123 years and was the founder of the Heavenly Masters sect).

Interestingly enough, the main controversy which overshadows the cult of the Jade Emperor has nothing to do with the legitimacy of his title Lord On High.   Even

張道陵

Chang Tao-ling

Buddhists and Confucians recognize his lofty position. The real controversy lies in the question as to *why* he was originally introduced into the Taoist pantheon.

Taoism is without question the most paradoxical of teachings. There is such a vast array of gods, immortals, deities and spirits that no one text has ever attempted to record them, not even the official documents of Taoism, the *tao tsang*. On the other hand, to be Taoist requires no belief in a Supreme Being or any particular heavenly deity. All celestial inhabitants may be regarded or disregarded at your discretion. The Taoist would look upon such beings as we might view extraterrestrial beings, having no real importance concerning our life. For the Taoist, God as some supreme attendant, as in the Christian sense, would be a rather amusing, if not totally erroneous belief. Supreme Beings, in the main, would be more a symbol or mythic image, representing one or another spiritual aspect within yourself, rather than something external.

The popular belief is that the Taoists needed both public and imperial patronage and so introduced the Jade Emperor as both an object of veneration and meditation, not unlike the Buddhist Pure Land practices surrounding *Amitabha Buddha* (Buddha of Infinite Light) and *Kuan Shih Yin Bodhisattva* (Contemplator of the World's Cries). To a lesser degree it gave them something to compete with against all the popular Confucian rites and ceremonies.

Interestingly, the Buddhists claim that the Jade Emperor is now waiting in the Tusita Heaven with Maitreya Bodhisattva (the next or future Buddha to enter our world), studying the Buddhadharma.   Because of his inconceivable and limitless past merits, the Jade Emperor is now serving as Supreme God until his introduction as a Bodhisattva into this realm of form and desire to teach joy, the dharma of

Maitreya.   But then the Buddhists usually took the stance that all accomplished Taoist immortals, sages and divine beings were actually transformation bodies of Buddha's disciples and/or a particular transformation of a Bodhisattva. The best example is Lao Tzu who is thought to be none other than Mahakasyapa, the first patriarch of Ch'an Buddhism (Zen). It was he who was first enlightened by the wordless teaching after seeing Buddha twirl a flower in his hand, and he is now deep in samadhi within the Chicken Foot Mountains awaiting Maitreya's entrance into this realm.

There is an on-going dispute that religious Taoism was nothing more than a competitive ploy, created to steal away Buddhist patrons and regain imperial favor, thus making them the more powerful force in spiritual circles.

Some of these charges may indeed be true, but it is quite difficult to generalize this and consider that Taoism was so well organized during this period that an orchestrated coup took place. It appears to be more a matter of various Taoist representatives acting independently. Likewise, many Taoist figures and communities probably either had no knowledge of these matters or if they did were more likely unconcerned, preferring their solitude and wishing to avoid any political involvement.

Over time Taoism did come to borrow a great deal from both the Pure Land and Secret Sect of Buddhism, but Ch'an Buddhism borrowed in a similar fashion from the Complete Reality (*chuan chen*) sect of Taoism.   It is very clear too that Taoism also improved itself philosophically through the *prajna* teachings of Buddhism. Taoism originally only spoke of things which were associated with the nature of voidness (*sunyata* in Buddhism). In the end both teachings benefited from each other. An old Chinese saying reads,

Lao Chun (Lao Tzu)

"To tell the difference between a Buddhist and a Taoist, is like trying to point out the differences between the feathers of one Mandarin duck and another". The semantics differed, but practices were mostly identical.

Explanation of the Terms within the Title

Yu Huang (The Jade Emperor)

The most important question concerning the origin of this text is whether or not the text existed before the popularization and deification of the Jade Emperor. His name is only mentioned in the title of the text, not in the text itself. Therefore it is quite possible that the text did exist before the Sung dynasty and that sometime during or after his deification under the Emperor Hui Tsung his name was attached to the title of the text.

The sixth line of the text refers to the *Shang Ti*. This reference is thought is to be to the Jade Emperor. But it must be remembered that the term "Shang Ti" existed long before the introduction of the name Jade Emperor. Lao Tzu was also given the honorific title of Shang Ti, as were others in the Taoist mystical pantheon. Also, if taken in the plural sense it might mean the Three Pure Ones (*san ching*, the Taoist trinity).

The term Shang Ti was first used in China's antiquity as a title for the head of a clan. Only later was it applied to supreme beings. In connection with the Jade Emperor Shang Ti means, "the Lord on High" or "Sovereign of Heaven". He is the supreme authority of all other gods and deities. Earthly emperors were considered his sons, "Son of Heaven". The Shang Ti is a summation of all the various

The Jade Emperor granting an official post for a new immortal.

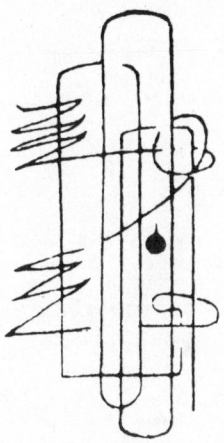

*Talisman of the
Jade Emperor*

Taoist hierarchies of gods. When one of them reaches a certain level of spiritual perfection and merit and the Jade Emperor decides to abdicate, then this god will replace him. There is also another group of mythic supreme beings called the *Jade Rulers*, consisting of Fu Hsi, Shen Nung and Huang Ti. However, these have no relation to the Jade Emperor in either lineage or in the history of his creation.

In the epic myth, *Journey to the West*, there are numerous references to the Jade Emperor and his Palace of Miraculous Mists. This novel of Chinese philosophical folklore, probably more than any other work in Chinese literature, popularized belief in the Jade Emperor, who with his retinue - a vast array of gods, immortals and spiritual beings - fights the evil spirits and forces within the heavenly and earthly realms. The references made to the Jade Emperor are too numerous to list here, as are the descriptions of his heavenly abode. Even though this celestial prime minister is not always regarded kindly by this primarily Buddhist novel, *Journey to the West* is well worth reading for anyone interested in Buddhism, Taoism or Chinese mythic culture in general. The novel, written by Wu Cheng'en (Ming dynasty), is on the one hand an anthology of Chinese folklore and a catalog of sorts of the various and numerous spiritual beings; from another perspective, it is a metaphor on the progression of spiritual cultivation (an integration of Buddhist, Taoist and Confucian methods). We all indeed carry within us aspects of either the Monkey King, Friar Sand, Pig, Horse, or even Hsuan Tsang the monk.

Indeed it would be hard to imagine that anyone could understand Chinese spiritual thought without having read this work thoroughly. For beyond the amusing children's tale lies both a very profound and mystic message for those engaged in spiritual cultivation.

Taoism is not a teaching about mysticism, it *is* mysticism. Taoism, as one soon learns through study and practice, is paradoxical, at least to the western way of thinking. There is no paradox to the Chinese mind. For the western mind to effectively understand and practice Taoism, there must be a realization that in reality it holds to no Supreme Being, recognizing only *Tao*, which is the primal spirit (*yuan shen*) in each of us, as the source of all things, an impersonal creative force. The mysticism, the Jade Emperor and all the various spiritual beings are in the final view simply symbols, real and yet unreal. A true Taoist would have no difficulty in choosing to view the Jade Emperor as the Supreme Lord of Heaven, but in the same breath equate this august figure as just a symbol of *yuan shen*. To the Taoist there is no contradiction in these two seemingly opposing views - one being an outer expression of religious practice, and the other, a self-empowered, internal expression of spirituality devoid of religious tenets.

The underlying doctrine of Taoism is that Man and Heaven are but reflections of each other and are One, for in each human lies both a Heavenly Spirit (*hun*) and Earthly Spirit (*p'o*). Therefore, to the Taoist there is no problem in religious practice. There is a problem when one thinks that this is the only means of spiritual enlightenment. The utilization of a personal God has never been something foreign to Taoism, but on the same hand it was never something taken as a final answer or as a reality. The practice and philosophy of *The Yellow Court Classic* (Huang Ting Ching) is evidence enough about the acceptance of supreme deities and religious practice in Taoism. I've never found much credence in the contemporary academic view that there is a separate religious and philosophical Taoism - Taoists hold both views without contradiction.

In the *Chuang Tzu,* which is a doctrine of the unconditioned nature of all things, there is a verse that relates to this question of God/Creator: "There appears to be a True God who does interact, yet there is no evidence of his existence." To Chuang Tzu, God is suspect. A personal God, who influences human life, even in the form of the Jade Emperor, is totally out of sync with his philosophy. Yet he admits to the appearance of a True God. In spite of his brief acceptance, Chuang Tzu focuses his beliefs on Nature (*Tao*) as creation itself, not on a creator in the personal sense.

Ko Hung (author of *Pao P'o Tzu*), commenting on Chuang Tzu's statement about a True God, denies the existence of a Supreme God, stating that "everything creates itself through Nature (Tao)".

Lao Tzu in the *Tao Te Ching,* which is a doctrine of the unproduced nature of all things, makes no distinction between Creator and No-Creator, claiming that "all things come from emptiness".

There are Buddhist equivalents of these two teachings. The *Vajra Prajna Paramita Sutra* (the Diamond Sutra) contains many of the same messages contained in the *Tao Te Ching.* The *Surangama Sutra* addresses many of the same issues addressed in *The Chuang Tzu.* It was these teachings, along with the *Platform Sutra of the Sixth Patriarch,* which really influenced Taoism.

It is now easy to see why Lu Szu-hsing considers the verse in the Tao Te Ching, "*keep to non-being, yet hold onto being*" as extremely important and why it has been the main paradox of Lao Tzu's philosophy. This verse can be interpreted in many ways, but for the purposes of understanding the perspective of the Jade Emperor it might be interpreted as, "keep to the idea of *no supreme* being, yet hold onto the idea of *a supreme* being". It is not in keeping with Taoism to view anything as absolute, supreme being or not. There is obviously an enormous difference between attaching to such

The Three Pure Ones

things in a one-sided manner and the acceptance of both sides of an issue. Extremist views tend to destroy themselves and converge into their opposite.

Ultimately, through Taoism, the ideal is to realize the

unity of heaven and man, hun and p'o, yin and yang, existence and non-existence, form and formless, production and non-production, conditioned and unconditioned. All these are *not two*. *Returning to the Source* in Taoism is not merely a statement on becoming an enlightened being, rather a statement on the actual reality of things. All things are One. It is only the illusionary mind of concepts and discriminations which envisions them as two.

Taoist thought is permeated with the notion that Man and Heaven are a unified whole; that the entire universe is contained within Man, that they are in essence one and the same. Again, in the *Huang Ting Ching* (The Yellow Court Classic) hundreds of spirit-gods are named and assigned to specific parts of the body, both internally and externally. The Jade Emperor's Court is in essence the "court of inner man". Taoism, seen in this light, is not dogmatic or even religious (at least in the western meaning of the term). Indeed the term "religion" is only a century old in the Chinese language, introduced by Christian missionaries. Originally, Buddhist, Taoist and Confucian ideas were simply referred to as "teachings". The notion of a dogmatic religion was entirely foreign to the Chinese until the intervention of western beliefs. So when the Taoist speaks of a Supreme God, the language is not the same as when a western Christian speaks of Supreme God. Whereas the Christian speaks of something totally external and distinct from himself, the Taoist is speaking of something internal and integral to his own being. Heaven and the Jade Emperor are external symbols reflecting his own inner being.

Spirituality to the Taoist is not religious, but rather a practical self-cultivation of three forces which embody Heaven, Earth and Man: *ching* (essence), *ch'i* (vitality) and *shen* (spirit). The restoration, accumulation and transformation of these three inner forces is what constitutes true spiritual illumination and immortality.

The Jade Emperor is part of the Taoist trinity, of which he is head. On his right side stands Tao Chun and on his left, Lao Tzu. They are commonly known as "The Three Pure Ones" (*san ching*). In more practical Taoist terms they are but symbols of the true trinity; primal (yuan) *ching, ch'i* and *shen*.

Yu Huang (The Jade Emperor), sometimes called "Jade Ruler" or "Pearly Sovereign" is for the most part identified with Brahma of Hinduism, Indra of Buddhism and to a lesser degree with the notions of God Almighty in Christian and Islamic traditions. He represents *shen* (spirit), *t'ien* (heaven), Primal Cause and present time.

Tao Chun (Sovereign of the Way), represents *ching* (regenerative force) and is identified with the Pole Star God. He represents *jen* (man), the interaction of yin and yang and time past.

Lao Tzu (Old Philosopher), represents *ch'i* (vital life-force energy) and is identified by the Taoist doctrine. He represents *ti* (earth) and future time.

This particular text refers to these three forces as the "supreme medicines", being the curative and preventive prescriptions for both human and spiritual ills, as well as the compound for the true elixir of immortality. The text is very brief, consisting of only two-hundred characters, arranged in four character couplets, which allowed the Taoist monk easy memorization and rhythmic recitation. The contents of the text cover a wide range of key verses and ideas crucial to the Taoist cultivator, reading more like a "crib sheet" to keep his mind on the essentials for attaining immortality, of which ching, ch'i and shen are the foundation.

Those unfamiliar with Taoist terminology, might view

Lao Tzu riding the back of a crane to visit the Eight Immortals.

this text as mere mystical "gibberish", but for the Taoist monk it is a tool for mindfulness. Indeed all Taoist practices, whether meditation, yogic inner alchemy exercises, visualizations, recitation of mantras or sacred texts and ceremonial rites, are in the end exercises in mindfulness, a self hypnosis of sorts.

The Jade Emperor's Mind Seal Classic was used daily by Taoist monks, especially those of the *Chuan Chen* (Complete Reality) and *Lung Men* (Dragon Door) sects, and recited on auspicious days by other sects. At *Po Yun Miao* (White Cloud Monastery) in Beijing, headquarters for these two sects, records show that this text was held in high esteem and that the novice *tao shih* (Taoist monk) had to memorize it during his one-hundred days training before ordination.

The auspicious days mentioned above consisted of the first and fifteenth days of each lunar month (these two are particularly auspicious because it is believed that the Jade Emperor sends the Four Heavenly Kings down to earth to check on everyone's behavior, thus you can acquire merit if they report your spiritual efforts); the ninth day of the first lunar month, which is the *Jade Emperor's Birthday*; the first day of the second lunar month, the *Festival of the Sun* (the day the sun visits the Jade Emperor's Palace of Miraculous Mists to determine the events of the coming year); and the sixth day of the eleventh lunar month, the *Jade Emperor's Anniversary on Becoming the Supreme Ruler.*

The Jade Emperor is, along with the Eight Immortals (*pa hsien*) the most popular of Taoist celestial beings, all of which are part of his court, along with a host of other spiritual beings and immortals. In popular tales however he is not always revered. He rarely intimidates the immortals of lesser rank and is often tricked by them into granting favors and promotions, not unlike earthly leaders. It is not a job to which most immortals aspire, as the powers of that position do have their limitations.

There are various interesting accounts as to how he became the Jade Emperor and three versions of his ascension. It is purely a matter of personal belief as to whether any of them are truthful. However, mythic history, usually told in metaphor, more often than not has its base in factual and documented history. There is always some truth embedded within the myth. Myth is the more valuable for its unique ability to open up and expand the mind, an exercise in imaginative powers which is so important to any spiritual endeavor, Taoist or otherwise. Dealing with "just raw facts" tends to block the mind from its creative instincts. Inner illumination is far more important to the Taoist than any worldly exercise of fact finding.

To the Taoist monk either of these accounts would suffice, since this august figure is symbolic, rather than personal. The first account is probably more fact than fiction, whereas the last two accounts are highly likely just "wild history". However, to the Taoist these last two might be more acceptable in that they have a higher inspirational value than the redundant first account - an attempt to just compile raw data, most of which could be just as mythical as the other two accounts.

Three Accounts of the Origin of
Yu Huang (The Jade Emperor)

The First Account

As Buddhism took hold in China during the Tang dynasty, the varying Taoist orders grew envious of the well organized Buddhist communities, which erected beautiful temples for their patrons. They became envious too of the Buddhist paraphernalia: their spiritual images, disciplines, rituals and volumes of literature. Especially during the Tang dynasty, Buddhism gained Imperial patronage, which put greater pressure on the Taoist representatives to get back into the court's grace and to regain the attention of the public at large.

So the Taoists began raising funds to build temples and monasteries, established the Taoist Canon, formulated rituals and began arranging their own hierarchy of spiritual beings. The beings were not necessarily new to Taoism, but this was the first sincere attempt to present them in an orderly fashion to the outside world. It was during this period that the top-knot was fashioned for all Taoist monks and priests. The Buddhists considered this just a ploy to differentiate themselves from the bald-headed Buddhist monks.

The Jade Emperor was created at this time mostly as a direct response and counterpart to the ever growing popularity of the Buddhist trilogies: *Buddha, Dharma* and *Sangha*; *Amitabha* (past Buddha), *Shakyamuni* (present Buddha) and *Maitreya* (future Buddha); and the Pure Land Sect's trilogy of *E Mi To Fo* (Amitabha Buddha), *Kuan Shih Yin* (Avalokitesvara) Bodhisattva and *Ta Chih Shih* (Mahasthamaprapta) Bodhisattva, which gained great popularity throughout China. In response the Taoists formulated their own triad called, "The Three Pure Ones", which consisted of the Jade Emperor, Tao Chun and Lao Tzu. Other triads were created but did not gain the equivalent broad acceptance. So it remains even today.

It is thought that the Jade Emperor, in his early life, was a member of the Chang clan. Almost all Taoists take Chang as their surname in order to connect themselves with the famous lineage of Chang Tao-ling of the Later Han dynasty, the founder of what is called "religious Taoism". So it is no great surprise that this lineage would be associated with him. Others propose that he was a well-respected magician and alchemist, and lived sometime during the early Tang dynasty.

However, his deification as Jade Emperor, Supreme Ruler, did not occur until 1116 A.D. in the Sung dynasty. He was deified, under some suspect conditions, by the Sung Emperor, Hui Tsung. It seems that an outcast Buddhist monk, Lin Ling-su, managed to convince the emperor to deify this Tang dynasty magician as Supreme Ruler, with the argument that the Buddhists were not indigenous to China and that it was not in the empire's best interest to condone and allow Buddhism to gain such popularity with the masses. However, this was not Lin's true motive. As soon as the deification took place Lin attempted to place himself at the head of this new Jade Emperor cult. He hoped thereby to crush the Buddhist influences prevalent in society and revenge himself against those Buddhist clergy responsible for ousting him. The Jade Emperor was deified and gained broad popularity, but Lin Ling-su never achieved his role as patriarch of the cult he had envisioned.

The Second Account

Long before the creation of the Jade Emperor triad of the
Three Pure Ones, there were other similar triads in certain
Taoist circles. The Jade Emperor, it appears, is just one in a
succession of Supreme Rulers. The first on record is *T'ai Yi*,
who abdicated in favor of *Huang Lao Chun*, who in turn
abdicated to *Yuan Shih T'ien Tsun*, and finally he abdicated
his throne to the Jade Emperor, who presently holds the
supreme position. However, it is said that when Maitreya
Buddha enters our world, the Jade Emperor will abdicate his
throne to another, as he will descend in order to serve this
Buddha. All the above was supposedly reported by the
Emperor Chen Tsung of the Sung dynasty (912 A.D.), who
presumably received an edict from the Jade Emperor himself
in a dream, informing him that he was about to take charge
of Heaven and reside in the Palace of Miraculous Mist, and
that the next earthly emperor was to deify him as *Yu Huang
Shang Ti* (Jade Emperor Supreme Ruler). Consequently,
Emperor Hui Tsung in 1115 A.D. deified the Jade Emperor
and began erecting temples and images in his honor.

The Third Account

The Jade Emperor is thought to be the son of an Emperor
named Ch'ing Ti, who had a consort called Pao Yueh-
kuang. She had reverently prayed to the gods for a son, as
the emperor still had no sons to inherit his throne. She did
indeed become pregnant, much to the happiness of the
emperor. The astrologers predicted a son would rule all of
heaven and earth. The child was most certainly a male. As
foretold, brilliant light had shot forth from his body and all
his physical features were perfect. The story goes on to claim
that as a youth he had great and far reaching intelligence and

very deep compassion for all living things. When he finally came of age and inherited his father's throne his acts of charity to the homeless, sick, impaired, orphaned and unjustly treated were very generous and kind. After his father's death he left the empire, resigning his throne, and travelled to the Pu Ming mountains to meditate, whereupon he achieved immortality.

After his departure from this world he was reborn again and for eight hundred successive lifetimes taught the common people about spiritual matters and doctrines. For another eight hundred lifetimes he returned to this world to cure the sick and instruct the common people on medical matters. For another eight hundred lifetimes he practiced unconditional compassion in both the hells and on earth. Lastly he descended to this world for yet another eight hundred lifetimes to patiently endure suffering. It was on the completion of these three thousand two-hundred lifetimes of spiritual practices that he finally achieved and became the first of the verified order of Golden Immortals. He was deified and ascended to the position of Supreme Ruler, called Yu Huang Shang Ti.

It is from this account that the Jade Emperor supposedly received his name, Yu (Jade). Since his father's name was Ch'ing (Pure and Bright) and his mother's, Pao Yueh-kuang (Moon Light Gem), the two names in combination symbolized *white jade* (yu).

Hsin Yin (Mind Seal)

Hsin Yin is a most difficult term to translate into English, which in turn also makes it difficult to explain. The term has three very profound and subtle interconnected definitions. The first is that of a deep and abstract experience of truth gained from the successful practice of meditation, which seals the mind forever from ever again entering a state of illusion and physical bonds. The experience here is abstract in that the realization experienced is wordless, and therefore cannot be communicated through language.

The second meaning relates to the procedure and experience of mind-to-mind transmission from teacher to disciple. In this sense of the term it is the teacher who seals the mind of the disciple on a particular doctrine or realization. This mind-to-mind transmission is again wordless. Though words might be used between them, it would prove quite impossible to translate those words into something comprehensible to anyone else. The disciple would be on the edge, so to speak, of a final realization and the teacher need only inject the proper catalyst for the disciple's transformation.

The third meaning is very ancient in both China and India, but was seen as a symbol, *wan tzu* (卍), a reverse swastika. In Buddhism it is used as a symbol depicting Buddha's heart. Taoism, very early on, incorporated it into a symbol of immortality. In China this symbol was a very old form of the character *fang* (方), which meant the four directions. Later fang became associated with wan (萬), the ten-thousand things (all phenomena). Hsin Yin is an interchangeable term with wan tzu, hence various translations could apply to this term, such as: "enlightened to all things" or "sealing the heart/mind within all phenomena".

Yin also carries the variant meaning of "mudra", a Buddhist term denoting a sacred hand position used for various reasons during meditation, recitation of a mantra or scripture and for warding off evil influences. So Hsin Yin here could likewise translate as "Mind Mudra", a sacred positioning of the mind.

Since the Taoists used wan tzu as a symbol for immortality, the title of this work could easily be translated as "The Jade Emperor's Classic on Immortality", however the meanings implied by "mind seal" are more appropriate in connection with the text, as the purpose of these sacred texts was to transmit wisdom which could lead to transformation.

Ching (Classic)

Ching means to thread together, such as strands of silk woven together make a fabric. The lines of the text, indeed the characters themselves, are thought to be woven together like strands of silk. There has never been a standard in English for the translation of this term, as it sometimes appears as canon, scripture, treatise or discourse.

玉皇心印經

上藥三品神與氣精恍恍惚惚杳杳冥冥存無守有頃刻而成迴

風混合。百日功靈默朝上帝一紀飛昇知者易悟昧者難行履踐

天光呼吸育青出玄入牝若亡若存綿綿不絕固蒂深根人各有

精精合其神神與氣合氣合體真不得其真皆是強名神能入石

神能飛形入水不溺入火不焚神依形生精依氣盈不凋不殘松

柏青青三品一理妙不可聽其聚則有其散則零七竅相通竅竅

光明聖日聖月照耀金庭一得永得自然身輕太和充溢骨散寒

瓊得丹則靈不得則傾丹在身中非白非青誦持萬遍妙理自明。

The Chinese Text for Yu Huang Hsin Yin Ching

THE JADE EMPEROR'S MIND SEAL CLASSIC

THE SUPREME MEDICINE HAS THREE DISTINCTIONS:
CHING (ESSENCE), *CH'I* (VITALITY) AND *SHEN* (SPIRIT),
WHICH ARE ELUSIVE AND OBSCURE.

KEEP TO *NON-BEING*, YET HOLD ON TO *BEING*
AND PERFECTION IS YOURS IN AN INSTANT.

WHEN DISTANT WINDS BLEND TOGETHER,
IN ONE HUNDRED DAYS OF SPIRITUAL WORK
AND MORNING RECITATION TO THE *SHANG TI*,
THEN IN ONE YEAR YOU WILL SOAR AS AN IMMORTAL.

THE SAGES AWAKEN THROUGH SELF-CULTIVATION;
DEEP, PROFOUND,
THEIR PRACTICES REQUIRE GREAT EFFORT.

FULFILLING VOWS ILLUMINES THE HEAVENS.
BREATHING NOURISHES YOUTHFULNESS.

DEPARTING FROM THE MYSTERIOUS, ENTERING
THE FEMALE.
IT APPEARS TO HAVE PERISHED, YET APPEARS TO EXIST.
UNMOVABLE, ITS ORIGIN IS MYSTERIOUS.

EACH PERSON HAS CHING;
THE SHEN UNITES WITH THE CHING;

THE SHEN UNITES WITH THE CH'I;
THE BREATH THEN UNITES WITH THE TRUE NATURE.
BEFORE YOU HAVE ATTAINED THIS TRUE NATURE,
THESE TERMS APPEAR TO BE FANCIFUL EXAGGERATIONS.

THE SHEN IS CAPABLE OF ENTERING STONE;
THE SHEN IS CAPABLE OF PHYSICAL FLIGHT.
ENTERING WATER IT IS NOT DROWNED;
ENTERING FIRE IT IS NOT BURNED.

THE SHEN DEPENDS ON LIFE FORM;
THE CHING DEPENDS ON SUFFICIENT CH'I.
IF THESE ARE NEITHER DEPLETED NOR INJURED THE
RESULT WILL BE YOUTHFULNESS AND LONGEVITY.

THESE THREE DISTINCTIONS HAVE ONE PRINCIPLE,
YET SO SUBTLE IT CAN NOT BE HEARD.

THEIR MEETING RESULTS IN EXISTENCE,
THEIR PARTING RESULTS IN NON-EXISTENCE.

THE SEVEN APERTURES INTERPENETRATE
AND EACH EMIT WISDOM LIGHT.

THE SACRED SUN AND SACRED MOON
ILLUMINATE THE GOLDEN COURT.
ONE ATTAINMENT IS ETERNAL ATTAINMENT.

THE BODY WILL NATURALLY BECOME WEIGHTLESS.
WHEN THE SUPREME HARMONY IS REPLETE,
THE BONE FRAGMENTS BECOME LIKE WINTER JADE.

ACQUIRING THE ELIXIR RESULTS IN IMMORTALITY,

NOT ACQUIRING IT RESULTS IN EXTINCTION.
THE ELIXIR IS WITHIN YOUR SELF,
IT IS NOT WHITE AND NOT GREEN.

RECITE AND HOLD TEN-THOUSAND TIMES.
THESE ARE THE SUBTLE PRINCIPLES OF
SELF-ILLUMINATION.

Lu Szu-hsing's Appended Verses

THE TWO IMAGES OF THE DRAGON AND TIGER ARE
UNIFIED THROUGH CH'I;
CHAOS BLENDING AS ONE.

IT IS NOT POSSIBLE TO ATTAIN THE ETERNAL JUST
THROUGH INVOCATION.

THE ELIXIR IS CALLED "GREEN DRAGON AND
WHITE TIGER";
THE ELIXIR IS THE NATURE OF NO-NATURE,
EMPTINESS OF NON-EMPTINESS.

EVEN IF YOU ARE UNABLE TO MAKE USE OF
THE SUBSTANCE,
YOU CAN CERTAINLY MAKE USE OF THE FUNCTION.

FREQUENTLY BOTH THE SUBSTANCE AND
CONDITIONS FOR THE SUBSTANCE APPEAR
TOGETHER,
ALTHOUGH THESE ARE NOT ALWAYS PERCEIVED
AS IDENTICAL.

THE ANCIENTS SAID, "*THE TERM EMPTINESS
EMBRACES THE ENTIRE TEACHING.*"

Commentary

The supreme medicine has three distinctions: *ching* (essence), *ch'i* (vitality) and *shen* (spirit), which are elusive and obscure.

The *supreme medicine* (shang yao), literally translates as, "the foremost healing herbs". The full meaning of this medicine includes not only the idea of a preventive or curative prescription for physical illnesses, but also the idea of a "wonder drug" for all mental and spiritual illnesses. These "supreme medicines" are not something external to the self, but rather the very forces which constitute your existence. These forces are considered by the Taoist as three primary functions within each human being: *ching, ch'i* and *shen*.

The three forces are normally referred to in Taoist works as "The Three Treasures" (*san pao*). It is the preservation and cultivation of these three that promotes health, longevity and immortality. Without these forces there can be no life, as it is their integration which constitutes existence. The degree of their abundance determines the level and quality of your health and the length of your life. Their transformation into "the elixir" brings about immortality.

It is the contention of Taoist philosophy that there is no reason for a person to ever suffer physical illness and that death itself, whether from old age or sickness, is also an unnecessary occurence. Illness and death occur because of the dissipation and destruction of the Three Treasures.

At birth everyone acquires a varying degree of *hsien t'ien* (Before Heaven) ching, ch'i and shen. After our birth we must then learn how to restore, gather and transform them. This is called, *hou t'ien* (After Heaven) ching, ch'i and shen.

The secret of health, longevity and immortality is not to damage the Before Heaven levels of ching, ch'i and shen. If they are damaged, we must learn how to *restore* them. The next step is to *gather* these three and then *transform* them into an elixir which confers immortality.

Before going on to an explanation of each of the three treasures it is worth noting that, within the *Tao Te Ching*, Lao Tzu speaks also of Three Treasures. However, the treasures of which Lao Tzu speaks have to do with moral conducts, not the forces of *hsien t'ien* and *hou t'ien*. In Chapter Sixty-Seven of the *Tao Te Ching* the term "san pao" is used, wherein Lao Tzu, speaking of the practice of *wu wei* (non-aggression), states that his three treasures are *frugality, compassion* and *mindfulness*. Looked at clearly, this expresses the idea of the restoration and gathering of ching, ch'i and shen.

An Explanation of Ching, Ch'i and Shen

CHING (Essence): Ching is normally translated as "sperm", but this is incorrect in the context of what the Taoists are speaking about, as women also have ching. In the broad sense, ching is the energy inherent within the reproductive process, the "giver of life". Ching is the reason we are born and equally the reason we die. Therefore, the Taoists believe reverently in both the preservation and conservation of ching. For when the ching is strong, vitality and youthfulness remain. In the male, too much dissipation will weaken the ching and thus shorten the life-span and produce illness. In the female, the ideal is to end the menstrual cycle in order to regenerate the ching. In both cases the ideal is to return to the period in our lives when we either did not dissipate sperm as males or menstruate as females. This is obviously the period of our lives when we were at the peak of our youthfulness and vitality, or had, as Lao Tzu puts it, "the pliability of a child".

But it is not only sexual dissipation which damages ching, as the Taoists believe that food and drink also play a major role. Food and drink enter into the blood stream and thus affect the five viscera and seven openings, leaving behind many impurities. To the Taoist, excessive eating and drinking is a sign of unrequited sexual desire. Monks, especially celibate ones, had to be very careful about their diet. But we must draw a distinction between excessive eating and obesity, as these do not have the same root cause. Obesity is a dysfunction of the Before Heaven ch'i (inherited). Excessive eating is a symptom of After Heaven ch'i (self-induced). Excessive eating and drinking is also considered the reason why a monk would enter states of oblivion during meditation. (I think we've all experienced that after a big meal). To the Taoist the end result of either excessive eating or emission is loss of vital energy. Great pains are undertaken to avoid this, so most Taoists choose celibacy and allow only one meal per day; others choose moderation and frugality. The goal of all Taoists is to eventually live off the "wind and dew", a poetic way of saying ch'i (breath) and saliva (the juice of immortality).

The term ching, as it is applied in the meaning of this text, makes use of three definitions: the energy which is the essence of procreation; the substances of sperm and menstrual fluids; and, when ching has been transmuted into a spiritual energy, the elixir of immortality. The Taoist classics usually refer to these three with the terms: *primal ching, turbid ching* and *true ching*. In general terms all these ideas equate to what is called *generative force* and/or *regenerative force,* in either the physical or spiritual sense. So to fully understand the term ching, as used in Taoism, there must be an understanding, not just of reproductive secretions and sexual energy, but of transformative energy as well. The Taoist view of sexual activity falls into three categories: *recreational, reproductive* and *restorative*. The restoration or repairing of ching falls under the third category, which is transformative, as only this aspect confers health, longevity and immortality.

The etymology of the character ching gives many clues as to why the Taoists choose this ideogram to represent the first of the Three Treasures. First of all, the main radical is *mi* (米), which symbolizes the idea of unhulled or uncooked rice, the natural state of the seed. Secondly, next to mi stands *ch'ing* (青), depicting the color of nature in the spring or growing stage, green. Ch'ing also stands for the white of an egg before the yoke develops. This ch'ing is made up of two symbols, *sheng* (生), meaning life and birth (⺮ is often a contraction of 生), and *tan* (丹), which can mean both the hue of young, sprouting plants and also "elixir." Sheng and tan combined express the idea of "elixir of life".

CH'I (Vitality): This term can be thought of as either "breath", "vital life-force" or "an inherent energy within the body". The various uses and meanings of ch'i, from breath to cosmic energy, make it a most difficult term to define. This definition will focus on personal ch'i.

All the self-cultivation practices for developing ch'i come down to one fundamental aspect, the warming of body fluids (blood, sexual secretions and body fluids). In the *I Ching* (Book of Changes) this is depicted by the image of the sixty-third hexagram, *After Completion*, which is represented by the diagrams of water (*k'an*) over fire (*li*).

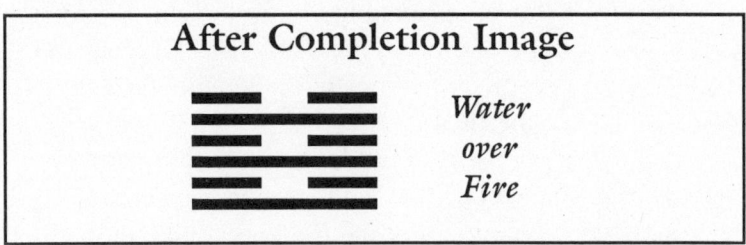

After Completion Image

Water over Fire

Using self-cultivation practices the blood is heated as it is stimulated through abdominal breathing; the blood then circulates more freely and begins heating the bones, turning them into marrow, which in turn causes the bones to be more pliable, yet strong and indestructible. The heat generated through abdominal breathing will also warm the other body fluids and the sexual secretions (ching). When all this occurs you can then sense free circulation of blood flow, the movement of ch'i rising from the *tan-tien*, along with an increased sense of vitality, stamina and lightness of body.

The human body, according to Taoist thought, contains five activities (*wu hsing*, the Five Elements). These are earth, wind, fire, water and metal. Earth represents the bones and flesh; wind represents the breath; fire, the heat (ch'i); water, the blood and other body fluids (ching); and metal, the elixir and spirit (shen). The process of refinement (*lien*) mentioned in many Taoist works, is simply a matter of: wind (breath) stimulating heat (ch'i), ch'i (fire) stimulating the blood (water) and blood (water) stimulating the bones and flesh (earth), to reach a state where the elixir is formed and the shen stimulated (metal).

In another analogy, when the breath is full the ch'i is abundant, when the ch'i is abundant the blood will circulate, when the blood circulates, the bones and flesh are nourished, and when the bones and flesh are nourished the elixir can be formed.

From the above explanations you will readily see why ch'i is so difficult to define, as there are many facets of ch'i. Ch'i is in the breath, in the heat, in the blood, in the bones and flesh and in the elixir.

The terms used, *full, abundant, circulate* and *nourished* should be explained further. "Full" means that you are breathing with the entire body and that the breath is focused in the tan-tien, like a bellows. "Abundant" is the stage of experiencing heat throughout the body. "Circulate" is the stage where the ch'i is experienced in the tan-tien and is circulating throughout the body, like steam driving the piston of an engine. Normally we must do something physical to get an increased blood flow, but in this case it is the ch'i circulating the blood flow. "Nourished" is the process whereby the stimulated blood flow and ch'i circulation begin permeating the flesh and bones with ch'i.

Etymologically the character ch'i is formed by two radicals. The first is ch'i (气), which represents several ideas, such as: a cloudy vapour, aura, spirit, breath, air and ether. The earliest meaning of this was "curling vapours which rise up from the earth to form the clouds above". The radical is derived from two symbols, *yun* (雲), clouds and *chih* (乙), the seed within man. The second aspect of ch'i is the radical mi (米), identical to that used in ching. From these the idea is expressed of "vapours which rise in the process of cooking rice".

 SHEN (Spirit): There are fundamentally three categories of "spirit energies": *ming shen* (bright spirit), *hsin shen* (mind/heart spirit) and *ling shen* (immortal spirit). These three are called *San Hun* (The Three Spiritual Energies): where, ming shen corresponds to *ch'i*, hsin shen to *ching* and ling shen to *shen*. Accumulating the ch'i causes the shen to become bright; when the ching is restored the shen manifests itself; and when the shen is transformed the shen is immortalized.

This is however a most difficult process to achieve, as we humans are affected by the Seven Emotions (*ch'i p'o*), which negate the transformation of our *hun shen* (or, san hun). The Seven Emotions are: happiness, joy, anger, grief, love, hatred and desire. All of these have negative effects on the progress of self-cultivation of the Three Treasures, which in turn affects our spiritual development.

The Taoist believes that when a human being is born to this earth they inherently acquire a *hun spirit* and a *p'o spirit*. The hun spirit is a representation of yang, heaven and immortality. The p'o spirit is a representation of yin, earth and mortality.

If we function during our lives totally within the Seven Emotions, then at death when the hun and p'o separate, we will return to earth as one type of *kuei* (ghost). The kuei does not survive long and fades away to become a *chi* (dead ghost). The hun on the other hand is in a sense immortal, as it survives a very long time, but will in time die if not united with a p'o spirit in which to return to earth and try again. If the feet are warm immediately after the point of death then the p'o descended; if the top of the head is warm then the hun ascended, a tell-tale sign of whether or not the person's spiritual practice bore any fruit. In brief, the only way out of this cycle is for the hun to undergo transformation as a true immortal.

When the shen is strong the mental faculties are sharp and lucid. Shen is expressed externally through the eyes, revealing not only a deep and profound intelligence, but a clarity and brightness of presence also. A strong shen enhances the ability of sight and mental insight. These are all aspects of attaining ming shen.

When the shen can be both retained internally and expressed externally then the shen can be released from the body at will, which is an effect of hsin shen. However, this is a very difficult stage to pass through because the shen, as years pass, becomes ever increasingly attached to the physical body. Usually only in a dream state can the shen be released to wander about. This is not truly an effect of hsin shen. Only willed and conscious release is a mark of this achievement.

When we are young the shen is strong and not so attached to the body, which is why we can have so many flying dreams in our youth. We feel immortal. We do not truly accept or comprehend death, old age and sickness. Time itself seems slower when young. Anyone can tell you how long summer vacation seemed to be in their childhood. However, in old age we become more material, clinging to forms and objects in hopes of prolonging life and, ultimately, avoiding death. The mind becomes ever more narrowed and unaccepting, time begins flying by ever quicker; days, months and years are perceived as becoming shorter and shorter. An old Chinese saying relates, "Pay heed young man, for in the twinkle of an eye you will be an old man."

However, if the shen is made strong, death is no longer a concern, time slows down and you become increasingly content with not only your lot in life, but with the world around you as well. All becomes tranquil. Like a youth, you are at playful ease. The attachment to the seven emotions ceases and the shen is free to interact with all conditions which arise. As the Taoist puts it, "you will remain unmoved even if Mt. Tai falls in front of you."

The derivation of the character shen is based on two radicals, *shih* (示) and *shen* (申). Shih is derived from *erh* (而), but this is yet an old form of *shang* (上), meaning heaven or the highest point, and *chuan* (川), which depicts those things which are suspended from heaven: sun, moon and stars. Combined, these radicals originally meant the influx of things from heaven which reveal transcendent matters to humans. Shen, the second radical is also a derivation of *t'ien* (田), a cultivated field. The extension of the central vertical stroke (丨), connotes a connective image between heaven and earth.

The Three Treasures are *elusive,* which means that seeking any of them as an object of possession will only result in them eluding you even further. They are not tangible substances or objects. The problem here is not a question of whether or not they are real or unreal, rather that our minds, in the deluded sense, cannot comprehend what the Taoists call, "the true emptiness of emptiness", or as the Buddhist Heart Sutra states, "*form is just emptiness, emptiness is just form.*" In analogy, this is like a person wanting to scoop up the reflection of the moon in the water with his hands, thinking that the reflection is the real moon. The Three Treasures are like this also, because through the experiences of cultivating them we attach ourselves to the sensations, only to discover that these are but reflections.

They are also *obscure,* which indicates that using the rational mind to somehow experience and analyze them without self-cultivation will only lead to further distortion.

Again, in analogy, this is like the man scooping up the reflection of the moon, but now when his hands actually touch the water the image of the moon is distorted. What at one point seemed so real is now revealed as an illusion. So the idea of *elusive* relates to our conception that these three treasures have form and are real; *obscure* relates to our experience of seeing them as empty and illusionary. These two extreme views are a natural progression for any who undergo self-cultivation. Then we swing back and forth between views of real and unreal, bouncing off the extremes in hopes of finding the middle. More on this later.

The Chinese characters for elusive and obscure are, *huang huang hu hu*, which were borrowed from Lao Tzu in the *Tao Te Ching*. However, Lao Tzu used them in the singular, huang hu. The doubling is just to be more expressive. As a compound huang hu means "the unconscious", "illusory" and "elusive". Lao Tzu used these two characters to express the idea of being lost and confused about spiritual reality and unreality.

Only the person who looks up and sees the true moon, not the reflected image, can transcend and awaken to the illusion of the moon in the water. Likewise, the depth of our attachment to the illusory moon can become almost unfathomable, for one illusion may yet be distorting another illusion. For example, you may see a small moon in a small body of water and a large moon in a large body of water. Each moon is relative to the body of water it is reflected in. Therefore, if you never see the true moon, your perception will always be conditioned by the illusory, reflected moon.

So the text begins by telling us that the medicine is for immortality, but then immediately warns us about the extremes of perception to which we may attach ourselves in trying to obtain these medicines.

Keep to *non-being*, yet hold onto *being* and perfection is yours in an instant.

This is the secret of immortality, but it is very difficult to understand because we are caught in the realm of duality. We cannot perceive anything without simultaneously deluding ourselves with its opposite. For example, we cannot know white without comparing it to black. Everything is like this: male/female, up/down, hot/cold. So the text here is revealing something very important, which is why Lu Szu-hsing considers it the most important line. This particular verse is taken from the *Tao Te Ching* and has been interpreted with various explanations.

In order to gain some understanding we must first examine the terms, *being* and *non-being*. In the Chinese the characters are *yu* (being) and *pu yu* (non-being). Yu means "to have" or "to exist"; pu yu means "not to have" or "not to exist". From this the idea is "keeping to non-existence, yet holding onto existence", or "keeping to non-emptiness, yet holding onto emptiness". Consider again the analogy of the person wanting to scoop the reflected moon from the water. When the person sees the reflected moon in the water and thinks it real, this person is attached to *being*. Conversely, when attempting to scoop the moon up, this person becomes attached to *non-being*. This is just how we as human beings perceive everything, either convinced that everything is real or that everything is unreal. But these are just extreme views and have nothing to do with this verse.

So how do we gain some understanding of this verse? First, know that things are "not-two". Things are not either non-being or being. In relation to the Three Treasures they are neither non-real nor real. However necessary such philosophizing might be, to really get to the heart of this verse

Accumulating light

we need to have some knowledge of both Taoist doctrine
and self-cultivation practices. To avoid becoming confused
the reader will need some fundamental knowledge of meditation and the internal energy doctrines of Taoism. The text

itself presents itself to the *tao shih* (ordained Taoist) from a level which takes for granted their knowledge of such matters.

In very early Taoist practices there were two processes necessary for the attainment of immortality. The first was called, *yang hou* (yang heat) and the second, *yin fu* (converging the yin). In more understandable terminology this can mean, the *seen* (yang) and *unseen* (yin). Yang ascends and yin descends. Within fire there is heat and within water is coolness. These ideas are usually expressed in Taoism as Green Dragon and White Tiger, but the teaching has been perverted into a gymnastics of breath control and mental visualizations. Almost all contemporary Taoist teachings are really just the process of yang hou, which is only the process of accumulating and circulating ch'i. This is not to say that yang hou is not a necessary process, but that it is only half the story.

In reference to Lao Tzu's verse, "hold onto being", yang hou is "being". Yin fu is then "keeping to non-being". Or as Lao Tzu also said, "from nothing comes something." What this means in connection with this text is that when we cultivate the Three Treasures on the level of restoration, accumulation and stimulation, we are only exercising the processes of yang hou, which is the process of refining ching and transmuting ch'i. However, when we refine the ch'i and transmute the shen this is yin fu or as the text calls it "instantaneous perfection".

However, how do we "keep to non-being and hold onto being" in the same instance? How can we possibly embrace something and nothingness simultaneously? Without involving ourselves in specialized jargon, we can paraphrase Lao Tzu's advice on experiencing or perceiving the Tao. If it (Tao) cannot be seen, then stop the looking; if it (Tao) cannot be heard, then stop the listening; if it (Tao) cannot be grasped, stop the grasping; if you cannot think your way to it (Tao), then stop the thinking. For as long as this "Tao" is viewed as an object or goal, it will be forever elusive and obscure.

We are like a person who is under the illusion of being imprisoned and frantically attempts to pry the door open to escape. Yet, in reality, this person is just breaking into a prison. This is synonymous with the process of yang hou, for immortality is still not attained. My teacher, Master Liang, would say humorously "yang hou is like eating, yin fu is like defecating. If you only practice yang hou you will stagnate, maybe burn up. So don't just eat and never defecate. Don't just borrow and never lend." Humorous, but true.

In Buddhism this same process was explained by Bodhidharma (Tamo) in the two works he left behind called, *Yin Chin Ching* (The Muscle Change Classic) and *Hsi Sui Ching* (The Marrow Cleansing Classic). The Yin Chin Ching reveals the yang hou process and Hsi Sui Ching, the yin fu. But few are those who can truly explain yin fu in the context of attainment, for it is not purely a question of intellectual understanding, rather of actual accomplishment, which is "uniting with the void." The Hsi Sui Ching in particular is not written in the form of method, rather in the perception of the effects.

In brief, this line of the text is referring to the Taoist goal of *Returning to the Source* and on perfecting the elixir of immortality. Which in analogy is the man scooping the moon from the water. However, in this instance he is no longer confused about the illusionary nature of the two (being and non-being), as he now perceives the truth of the source of the reflected and distorted moons, as well as being able to look directly at the True moon (True Nature). At this time he is instantly awakened and will never be confused by the two (being and non-being) again.

When distant winds blend together,
in one hundred days of spiritual work
and morning recitation to the Shang Ti,
then in one year you will soar as an immortal.

Distant winds is an aphorism for the ching, ch'i and
shen in the unrefined and unrestored state. *Blending together*
means that they have been transmuted into the "elixir of
immortality". This stage of practice is also called "setting up
the consciousness". It centers itself on working with the
light within the eyes, a result of having refined ching and
transmuting ch'i.

One hundred days of spiritual work is a reference to the
actual period of time for the ordination of a Taoist monk
(*tao shih*). Within this time frame the would-be monk is
required to establish within himself all the disciplines and
moral deportments necessary for the cultivation of immortality. One of these disciplines is what is commonly called
"Virgin Boy Training", which is one hundred days of pre-
serving and restoring the ching. It is thought in Taoism that
if a person undergoes this training their ching can be fully
restored to equal their ching prior to losing their virginity. It
would also reveal very quickly to the chief ordination monks
whether or not this person was suited to spiritual and
monastic life.

Another, far more profound viewpoint on this, comes
from the *Me Wang Ching* (Classic on Regarding the Pulses):
"When the ch'i of the primal spirit (yuan shen) has not yet
been experienced, the idea is to perceive that "one thing"
which is like a great weight dropping directly down into the
tan-tien to begin the completion of the elixir. Afterwards

continue breathing and let it join naturally, yet constantly be mindful of it and not for a moment let it go. This is the true meaning of "one hundred days of spiritual groundwork", which is just a term for the art of perfecting the elixir. One hundred days is only an approximate number."

Recitation refers to five primary texts which were memorized by the tao shih and chanted every morning: *Yu Huang Ching, San Kuan Ching, Chen Wu Ching, T'ai Shang Kan Ying Pien* and *Wen Ch'ang Ti Chun Yin Chih Wen*.

Shang Ti here is a reference to both the Jade Emperor and his entire court of celestial beings. When they witness the monk's sincere practice and devotion to the attainment of the Way, they would be moved to lend spiritual aid to the future immortal. In Taoism there is a saying which relates to this. "When a person finds the Way, heaven is gentle. When the Way is not found earth is harsh."

Then in one year you will soar as an immortal. The Taoist believes that it takes a human being about one year to enter this earthly realm and that it should take no longer to become an immortal, as both are just a transformation process.

There is another viewpoint on this line of the text, which is that it could read, "In one year an ascending immortal will appear". A spirit guide will come to aid the cultivator at a certain stage in his development in order to hurdle him past some very formidable obstacles.

However, in more practical Taoist terms this verse is more likely a reference to the notion that it is the shen which is released from the physical body. Since the shen retains the image of the body, exactly like that in the dream-state, it only appears to be flying. Actual physical flight is an entirely different subject in Taoism, as there appears to be two dis-

An Ascending (Sky Flying) Immortal.

tinct beliefs. Some only accept that it is the shen which is released and thus flies. Others accept the fact that it is the physical body which flies. We also find this in Buddhism. *Rsi* (immortals) are classified into five types: heavenly immortals, earth wandering immortals, spirit immortals, sky flying immortals and ghost immortals.

However, flying or soaring is an incidental term here in comparison to the term "immortal" (*hsien jen*). The term has such a wide usage in Taoism that it is difficult to give it a particular meaning. It has been used posthumously for many sages and yogins, and awarded as an honorific to those of old age. However, no matter the usage, to be an immortal has always been the goal of Taoists. Whether or not to be immortal meant actual physical flesh and blood transformation to eternal life, or immortality of the hun shen, or extraordinary long-life, the idea of immortality permeates all of Taoism.

Immortality is divided into three categories: the highest level is called "a heavenly immortal"; second highest is, "an earthly immortal", and the lowest is called "a corpse freed immortal". According to Ko Hung (author of the *Pao P'o Tzu*) those immortals of the highest grade can ascend their bodies directly into the Void, and are then classified as "Heavenly Immortal". Those of the middle grade retreat to the mountains to refine the elixir even further, and are termed "Earthly Immortal". The third type can only be freed from the body at death, yet the *shen* (spirit) remains intact, and are called "Corpse Freed Immortal". The highest grade becomes a heavenly official; the middle grade joins the earthly immortals on Mount K'un-lun; and the third grade enjoys longevity and *te* (virtue) on earth. Those who are destined to become heavenly immortals can achieve their aim even if serving in the military. Those to be earthly immortals can do so even if serving as a government official. The corpse freed immortal however needs to first retreat to the mountains or forest.

In the *Immortal Classic* (Hsien Ching) it adds that Heavenly Immortals can make gold from cinnabar, the elixir of immortality. Earthly Immortals can only make use of herbs, mushrooms, internal calisthenics (e.g., T'ai Chi Ch'uan) and breathing exercises (e.g., Tao Yin and Ch'i Kung). Those of the third grade can only maintain themselves through the ingestion of herbs. However, the practical basis and only requirement for the attainment of immortality lies in three fundamental things: the treasuring of ching, the circulation of ch'i and the taking of one crucial medicine (the elixir), which is produced from the first two. The secret is knowing how to treasure the ching and how to circulate the ch'i. There are numerous methods for both and you must be able to distinguish the profound from the shallow.

The creation of the immortal foetus

Through *purity* the ching is treasured; through *tranquility* the ch'i is circulated; through *emptiness* the shen is awakened. The ideas of purity, tranquility and emptiness are all within the mind. In Taoism the words "bathing" and "washing" are used frequently, but this is just a reference to these three processes. Some later Taoists, especially those of the hygiene schools, adapted these two words in the names for specific exercises, but the meanings are quite different.

Something should also be said here about the differences in the terminology of immortality and enlightenment, as so many of us confuse these two and tend to lump them into the same basket. The highest stage in Taoism is called *kung hsing* (Void Nature), called *sunyata* in Buddhism. This stage ends in the fourth heavenly realm above Mt. K'un-lun, but is still in the realm of form as it is only the nature of voidness, not voidness of itself. This is the level of heavenly immortals and is indeed enlightenment (*chio*), but not the level that Buddha attained and called, *annutarasamyaksambodhi*, which leads to *nirvana*, wherein all realms are surpassed and extinguished. Therefore, in the context of Buddhist and Taoist definitions of "awakened", the terms enlightenment and immortality are not always identical. Even so, kung hsing is a very high state of attainment. Earthly immortals do attain a state of awakening (*wu*), but are limited to realizations concerning this realm of form and the unrealness of it. Corpse Freed immortals are not necessarily awakened but do acquire a great deal of wisdom. In brief, heavenly immortals are those which leave this earth and function somewhere within the Jade Emperor's Court; earthly immortals are usually referred to as True Men (*chen jen*); and, Corpse Freed immortals are those coined as Sages (*sheng*).

The term immortal (*hsien*) is also used in China rather freely. Indeed it is used in so many variant descriptions that even a learned Taoist would find difficulty in defining it in a definitive manner. Old men are frequently called, in the honorific sense, "old immortal". Taoist monks, whether accomplished or not, are usually referred to as "immortal". There is also the problem of those magician-alchemist Taoists who sought immortality only through the transmutation of base metals, herbs and plants. I do not know that such formulas really existed or worked, and if so, I would be hard pressed to understand how awakening or enlightenment could be a direct effect of such formulas.

The sages awaken through self-cultivation; deep, profound, their practices require great effort.

Even if you were born with many inherent spiritual penetrations you must still cultivate yourself, or you will lose them. No one is exempt. Anybody seeking to be an immortal must undergo the spiritual work, which is very difficult. However, the difficulty is really only in the repetition of practices. The text states that the work required is deep and profound, meaning that it must be investigated and thought out very well, through both study and practice. You can't just pick up a book on Taoism, read it and think you've got it. You must study intensely every day. Without great patient effort and diligent study you cannot accomplish it. A Ch'an adage reflects this well, "Cultivation is like climbing up a hundred foot greased pole; enlightenment is synonymous to reaching the top of the pole and then making a great leap upward." Climbing the greased pole takes great effort, but leaping from it takes not only great courage, but wisdom as well.

During a discussion long ago with Master Liang, a most accomplished "old rogue" as Chuang Tzu might call him, he told me, "If you truly want to be an immortal, then simply give up your mortal ways." Thinking this over we can see how very arduous this could be. It sounds so simple, yet it is deep and profound. It sounds easy, yet indeed it is difficult. For how many of us in truth could apply ourselves to the required spiritual work for even one day, not to mention one hundred days? Very, very few I think. How many for that matter could do it steadfastly for one hundred days, not to mention an entire lifetime? Even less I'm sure. Most of us, simply give up anything after a little bit of suffering or inconvenience and fall quickly back into our mortal pleasures.

Sometimes I think our modern society has redefined the term 'Three Treasures" to mean, "sex, drugs and rock'n'roll". The Taoists have a saying, "it is easy to do bad, but most difficult to do good." If someone says, "hey, let's go out and get a drink", we follow without the least bit of resistance. However, if they said, "hey, let's go out and help the homeless", much thought and excuse would intervene. Attachment to the desire for acceptance has always been a human roadblock. The desire for acceptance is really none other than conformity and the Taoists have always sought to rid themselves of that trait.

On a more humorous, yet truthful note, Master Liang's teacher, Cheng Man-ch'ing, was said to possess Five Excellences: painting, medicine, calligraphy, poetry and T'ai Chi Ch'uan. Master Liang claims that before he met his teacher he also had five perfections: drinking, drugs, womanizing, gambling and smoking. Afterwards, given a diagnosis of only two months to live at age forty five, he took up T'ai Chi Ch'uan and out lived even his teacher. So today he lives to tell people to give up their bad habits and renew themselves each and every day.

The main problem is that people need a real reason, usually life threatening, to give up what they consider a pleasurable habit. People usually don't change their modes of behavior without being almost forced into it. "To remove a mountain is easy, but to change a man's temperament is most difficult", and this is the reason why the "sages awaken through self-cultivation; deep, profound, their practices require great effort", because the practice is ultimately about changing themselves.

Even though the text here speaks of practice, this does not imply fanaticism nor physical and mental exertion, which would just be the opposite extreme of being unmindful and slothful. The Middle Way (*chung tao*) is in essence "hitting the bull's eye". Being extreme about anything only ends up in being led off course. A Chinese adage, "home for one day, gone for three" means that it is better to practice every day for one hour, then to practice for one full day and quit for three.

The word practice in English carries two meanings. The first is something we do repeatedly to get better. The second, is an occupation or hobby, such as a doctor, who performs what he knows in a repetitive manner. Taoist practice is like the latter.

The first meaning implies too much stress on goal orientation, competitiveness and ego, which are none other than aggression, a negative attribute for the Taoists. The latter however is more in keeping with the idea of *wei wu wei* (active non-aggression). Simply use the knowledge at hand, practice it, and gradually perfection will be achieved without the ego of achieving. Chuang Tzu states, "knowledge is unlimited", so don't think that you need to know everything before practicing, no one can. Success is in the doing, not in the procrastinating.

You must never shun either the study of your practice nor the contemplative examination of it. Albert Einstein rightly said, "Practice without theory is blind; theory without practice is sterile". The practice is arduous only in that it must be repetitive, day after day, night after night. With every success continue to practice, keep refining it.

Unwavering practice is indeed most difficult. Your own sincerity will lead you to the right door. Simply endure the repetition, then teachers, books and experiences all come about in their due time.

Another problem, indigenous to us Westerners in particular, is what Master Liang coined as "hippie-ippy Taoism", wherein laziness and lack of ambition is justified with the sixties notion of wu wei. Nothing could be more erroneous. True Taoist practice takes great discipline, endurance and patience. Just to lay back, sleep, cook rice and call it wu wei is most absurd.

Fulfilling vows illumines the Heavens.

It is said that "when you are in harmony with the Way, heaven is gentle". To fulfill a vow means to eradicate greed. Some Taoists make vows of poverty, silence, charity, service, celibacy or practice. To fulfill a vow means that some form of sacrifice has to be made, thereby ridding the mind of greed. The heavenly beings are said to get excited about those who undertake such tasks because to them it means that there is someone down here on earth who may join them in the · future. They prepare by lighting up the various palaces in heaven so that the cultivator can find it. Really I don't know if this is true or not. I heard it somewhere and thought I'd share it. The *I Ching* says, "All things of this earth are but archetypes in heaven". If there is war on earth, then the heavenly beings are fighting with heavenly demons, and so on.

What I do know to be true is that fulfilling vows illumines your mind. There is a definite clarity and light which results from this. Once I read a story about a monk who vowed to bow to the ground every three steps from temple to temple for three years in earnest, so that he could transfer spiritual merit to his parents after their death. Really a hard job. An onlooker asked the monk, "Why are you bowing like that?" The monk answered, "Because I'm grateful." "Grateful for what?" the onlooker questioned again. "Ultimately, nothing", the monk responded, "but it is such a bright and wonderful state of mind." If you understand this monk's meaning you will know why fulfilling vows illumines the heavens.

Breathing nourishes youthfulness.

This is so simple that it protects itself from being discovered. In fact it is so simple that unless someone tells you, you would never even think of it and when someone tells you it isn't believed. Chuang Tzu talked about it quite clearly, but everyone still runs around looking for that big secret. Lao Tzu told us not to leave our own house, but off we go on a thousand mile journey. The breath is mind; the mind is breath. Even many well known Taoists "put legs on a snake" and make breathing techniques complicated and further confuse the issue by implying a secrecy to the technique. Not that all these techniques and teachers *per se* are neither right or true. Some techniques are indeed useful in various situations. But to acquire and maintain youthfulness and tranquility is quite simple.

First you need to understand the term "natural breathing", which is really not a method at all. The term is trying to make clear the idea of breathing as we did as a small baby. Lao Tzu's question, "Can you attain the pliability of a child?", is a reference to this subject. Lao Tzu also said, "the whole of cultivation is in subtraction, not addition." Taoism focuses on reversal, restoration and rejuvenation to that state when we were a child, to youthfulness.

During the span of our life our breath constantly rises upwards, until at death the breath finds itself in the throat, not in the lower abdomen as it was during childhood. When young our cheeks are reddened, joints slightly bent, the bones soft, the body is warm and the breath is "natural" and concentrated in the abdomen. As we get older our cheeks pale, joints stiffen, bones become brittle, the body chills and the breath is concentrated in the chest. The Taoist seeks to reverse this and return to a more natural state of health and vitality.

When a child breathes there are no thoughts of fixing the breath in the abdomen, the breath is there naturally. The child also breathes fully with the abdomen, meaning the entire stomach expands and contracts slightly so that it functions like a bellows or balloon, not like those stomach pushers who just expand and contract the front of the stomach. This is only half breathing. The breath should be felt on the lower spine and on both sides of the lower abdomen as well.

The big secret is really no secret at all. All that need be done is focus the mind on the tan-tien, not the breath; the breath will follow the mind. Mind does not follow the breath.

To breathe naturally you must allow the breath to become deep, slow and harmonious. This is something which cannot be forced by a method or technique. Picture your mind as a dirty glass of water. The more you agitate it the cloudier it becomes. However, if you just let the glass sit, the debris will gradually filter to the bottom and the water will become clear again. Trying to make the breath deep, slow and harmonious is like stirring the water; the breath cannot be natural because you are forcing it. But just by letting it go, it will sink of its own accord and become natural. So natural breath means just that, to be natural. How to be natural? Calm the mind, empty your mind, don't fill it with techniques and schemes. As the mind settles so will the breath, but you cannot force this to happen, it can only come about naturally. Eventually, when the mind and breath settle, the breath will be almost undetectable, like Chuang Tzu's "withered log and dead ashes" analogy.

Yin Shih Tzu, a famous Taoist contemporary, relates in his work that, "when I left the breath alone to sink into the tan-tien of its own accord then the ch'i rose upwards and circulated throughout all my limbs." His only technique was simply, "abiding by the tan-tien", meaning he only focused his attention on the tan-tien, not his breath. The T'ai Chi Ch'uan Classics relate the same principle of not focusing on the breath as it will only result in obstructing the ch'i.

There are many techniques related within Taoist works concerning breathing exercises, such as holding the breath, embryonic breath, reverse breath, tortoise breath. All these exercises are valuable. However, natural breathing should be considered both the basis and the culmination of all the techniques. Without acquiring natural breath the other methods are merely fascinating toys and lead nowhere except for some psychological and possibly physical ills. The other techniques become valuable only after you have experienced and can consciously control the circulation of ch'i, not before. As Master Liang related, "don't speak of defecation to a starving man; don't speak of winter to the mayfly." The first and biggest step is to acquire natural breath. Don't bother with other forms of breathing until you've accomplished it. Don't be like the man in the Ming dynasty who bought a thousand books but could not read.

Breathing is not a secret, or if it is, then it is an "open secret". For natural breathing occurs naturally, not by force or invention.

Departing from the Mysterious, entering the Female.

This verse comes directly from Chapter Six of the Tao Te Ching: "The Valley Spirit never dies, it is called the Mysterious Female. The gateway of the Mysterious Female is the source of Heaven and Earth. It has been with us constantly; use it as you will, it is never exhausted."

In the *Recorded Sayings of Master Ta Ma* it is said, "The Mysterious (*hsuan*) represents heaven, ching (essence) and the nose. The Female (*p'in*) represents earth, blood (and ch'i) and the abdomen. Hsuan is the father of ching, and p'in is the mother of ch'i. So that which departs from the father is ching, that which enters the female is ch'i. Within each person there is the Mysterious Female. Everyone can create a spiritual embryo. The Valley Spirit refers to yang shen (pure spirit); with just one drop of yang shen uniting with the ching and ch'i, the spirit embryo is born."

Again, in paraphrase, by treasuring the ching, circulating the ch'i and taking one crucial medicine, immortality is achieved. The crucial medicine is yang shen or the Valley Spirit as Lao Tzu puts it. But the big question is "what is yang shen?" Really there is no need to ask because it has been with you all the time. However, until the ching is restored and the ch'i circulates it remains hidden and cannot form the elixir of immortality. This is like having a pot of water and a stove, but for one reason or another you never connected the two as being components for making steam. Making steam may have seemed like magic long ago when it was first discovered. So too does creating a spirit embryo seem like magic to those who do not treasure ching and circulate the ch'i and cannot see them as components for immortality. Saint Augustine aptly said, "There are no miracles, just unknown laws of nature."

圖 神 出

Releasing the spirit (shen)

It appears to have perished, yet appears to exist. Unmovable, its origin is mysterious.

This is referring to the Valley Spirit or yang shen. We all have a sense that there is some spiritual aspect within us, yet we cannot touch it, smell it, hear it, taste it or see it. So we assume it doesn't exist, yet because we sense it with our minds and hearts we assume it exists. However, it is within each of us and is unchanging and never dies, unmovable. But as to where it comes from even Lao Tzu admitted ignorance, "I do not know its origin", so he just made up a name, Tao.

This spiritual aspect is what the alchemists call the "spirit embryo", a spiritual pregnancy of sorts. This embryo is also described by the earlier passage, "keep to non-being, yet hold onto being", which is how the Taoist views this inner spiritual aspect of himself. Here, the view is that it appears not to really exist (in substance), yet simultaneously it does exist (in function).

This is what Lu Szu-hsing meant in his appended verses, *"Even if you are unable to make use of the substance (non-being), you can certainly make use of the function (being). Frequently both the substance and conditions for the substance appear together. Although these are not always perceived as identical."* Substance means primal essence (Before Heaven or pre-birth condition); function is the "turbid ching" (After Heaven or post-birth condition). Substance creates the spirit embryo; function creates human life, but can be restored to form the elixir and return to primal essence. Sometimes the primal essence (Before Heaven) and the conditions for it (After Heaven) appear simultaneously - a living spirit embryo.

Not always being perceived as identical means that we are normally perplexed by the idea that the primal essence (Before Heaven) and turbid ching (After Heaven) are essentially identical. Meaning, the inner essence and outer manifestation of all things are, in the end, identical. Just as the leaves and branches of a tree are identical with *treeness*. We all have the medicine of immortality within us (the substance), yet we cannot see that our very existence is a manifestation of (the conditions) of immortality.

Moreover, the accomplished adept, on forming and realizing this embryo, understands that it was always there, eternal. Yet, even with this knowledge and experience, the origin of it eludes him. This is like the discussion of what came first, the chicken or the egg. We can see the chicken, we can see the egg, we can even understand the transformation and impregnation, but we cannot know where any of it first originated. Lao Tzu just called it Tao for lack of knowing what to call it. Buddha told us not to think about it, that beginnings and endings are the illusory nature of mind.

Each person has ching; the shen unites with the ching and the shen unites with the ch'i. The breath then unites with the True Nature. Before you have attained this True Nature, these terms appear to be fanciful exaggerations.

Most of this has already been explained, except that the True Nature is a name for your primal spirit (yuan shen) within the context of having attained immortality. Previous to this state you are not aware of your True Nature, which is why the text emphasizes that if you have not attained to this True Nature then all these words and names are nothing but fantasy and exaggerations.

Uniting the breath with the True Nature is a state in meditation where breath is no longer just a physical function. The mind moves the breath in such a subtle manner that it is almost imperceptible, yet the breath is much fuller. This is the very beginning of the creation of the spirit embryo and the first stage in releasing the p'o spirit's control over the physical body. Once this stage is experienced there will be no more doubt about the shen or the existence of spiritual energies within yourself. Some works refer to this as the "one breath" (*i ch'i*) or Before Heaven breath, as it is the breath you possessed before you were born.

The shen is capable of entering stone; the shen is capable of physical flight. Entering water it is not drowned; entering fire it is not burned.

In the *Chuang Tzu* we find in Chapter One a discussion between Chen Wu and Lien Shu about a man living on Ku She Mountain who had skin like ice and snow, gentle and innocent as a young girl. He did not eat any of the five grains, but drank wind and dew. He could climb upon clouds and mists, ride flying dragons and wander beyond the four oceans. Chien Wu thought all this nonsense, but Lien Shu reprimanded him. Lien Shu explained that a man like the one on Ku She Mountain could not be harmed by anything. That even if flood waters reached the sky, he would not be drowned. If all the metals and stone of the earth were melted by drought, he would not be burned.

The underlying principle here is that an immortal has control over the five elements, rather than the elements controlling him. The shen here is referring to the mind, but in the state of an immortal the mind controls the body, or in Taoist terms, the hun spirit has conquered the p'o spirit. In the mortal state the body, for the most part, controls the mind, which is to say that the p'o spirit overwhelmingly influences your actions.

The shen depends on life-form and the ching depends on sufficient ch'i. If these are neither depleted nor injured, the result will be youthfulness and longevity.

Without a physical body within which the shen can unite with the ching and ch'i; without sufficient ch'i for the ching to unite with, there could be no immortal foetus or elixir of immortality to which to give birth. For this reason the hun and p'o need each other. The body is like the cauldron in which the mixture may be refined, but once complete shen no longer needs a life-form. However, the key statement here is that if the ching and ch'i are not depleted or injured then youthfulness and longevity will ensue. Youthfulness and longevity are important to the Taoist in that there will be added years in which to form the elixir and youthfulness will provide the vitality and stamina needed for the endeavor. Just to live a long time is of no value to the Taoist unless good health accompanies it.

These three distinctions have one principle, yet so subtle it cannot be heard.

The three distinctions are ching, ch'i and shen. The one principle is that through experiencing emptiness (returning to the void) immortality is achieved. But how would anyone ever know about it unless they were told? The formula is that subtle and abstruse. However, even if you hear it there is no guarantee that you can make use of it. Because first you must know how to treasure the ching correctly, how to circulate the ch'i correctly, how to unite them with the shen. Even if all this is accomplished there is still the problem of refinement and transformation. So it is no easy task. As Li Ching-yun (a contemporary Taoist reported to have lived two hundred and fifty years) stated, "Forming the elixir is easy in comparison to having first put an end to the Seven Emotions (*chi p'o*)." The text is indeed talking about some very subtle conditions to be mastered.

Their meeting results in existence, their parting results in non-existence.

When the Three Treasures come together we attain life; in their refinement and transformation we attain immortality. When they separate or become exhausted we die.

This line can also be interpreted to mean that when the hun and p'o unite there is life, when they separate each goes their own way and soon dies. Therefore, the Taoist seeks immortality in order to preserve the hun spirit, thus preventing the p'o spirit from becoming a demon or ghost and having to undergo the long transmigration period of uniting the hun and p'o just to endure human suffering over again.

This is also a reference to when the sun and moon unite in the Golden Court; or when the Green Dragon and White Tiger are sublimated in the cauldron; or when lead and mercury are transmuted into gold; or when yin and yang return to Tao.

The seven apertures interpenetrate and each emit wisdom light.

The *seven apertures* are the two eyes, two ears, two nostrils and the mouth. (*The nine openings* include these in addition to the anal orifice and the sexual organ orifice. These last two are not included here for the reason that they are to be closed off from any dissipation of energy). The seven apertures are the holders of the *six senses*, sight, sound, smell, taste, touch and thought. Each of these senses also has a consciousness, which can interpenetrate any of the others. The eyes can smell, the mouth can hear, the nose can feel, the mind can touch and so on. This is really true. In all there are eighteen sense realms: six sense organs, six sense consciousnesses and the objects of the senses. It is only because of our discrimination of the senses, objects of sense and the attachment to the physical organs themselves that we cannot experience interpenetration of these consciousnesses. We, and we alone, have imprisoned ourselves within those sensations of sense. The immortal is free of those discriminations and attachments, and so can use any of those consciousnesses in whatever fashion desired.

The immortal's mind clearly sees that these sense organs are all empty and can thus illuminate both the consciousnesses and the objects of those senses. This is the state of Nature Void discussed earlier.

When you enter this state of Nature Void the seven

apertures can emit light, or wisdom light as it is properly called. To explain this phenomena all we must understand is what happens when we shut our eyes. Do colors appear or not? Of course they do. When we dream we also see colors and lights. Where do these colors and light come from when we have closed off our organ of sight? From the consciousness of sight. When dreaming we may close off the sense organs, but the sense consciousnesses still function and thus produce objects of sense. Therefore, the immortal understands that not only are objects of the senses illusionary and false, but that the organ and consciousness are also, and is thus left with the experience of Nature Void.

This is what Chuang Chou spoke about in chapter two of his work (*The Chuang Tzu*). "*I, Chuang Chou, dreamt once that I was a butterfly flitting about, going anywhere as I liked. I had no knowledge of a Chuang Chou. But suddenly I awoke and became the usual Chuang Chou again. Now I don't know whether it really was Chuang Chou dreaming he was a butterfly, or that the butterfly is now dreaming to be Chuang Chou. I suppose there must be some distinction between this Chuang Chou and the butterfly, but this is what is meant when we say that things undergo transformation.*"

A butterfly is used in Taoism to symbolize the metamorphosis of a mortal being into an immortal being, just as a caterpillar transforms into a butterfly. Chuang Tzu uses this story in a very clever manner, revealing that he underwent this transformation and realized that the consciousnesses of the senses were empty and false, along with the organs of sense and objects of sense. For if those senses, in either the organ state, consciousness state or object state were true and real, then how could Chuang Chou be unaware of dreaming he was a butterfly and likewise how could the butterfly be unaware of Chuang Chou?

The Seven P'o Spirits and Three Hun Spirits

Moving on, when you realize that these senses, their consciousnesses and objects, are empty, the mind becomes very bright and light is actually emitted from each of the seven apertures. This is wisdom light, which comes from illuminating the true nature of the six senses. It is much like opening the curtain in the morning where light rushes in to fill the room. But in this case it is reversed, as the brightness of your mind shines outward.

In meditation practice, many undergo the experience of seeing what seems like a thousand tiny lamps suspended inside the top of the head, along with an extreme sense of joy. This is neither enlightenment nor transformation. You should not attach to the experience. This light shining within the mind however is an indication of the existence of wisdom light. It cannot shine outwards because there is still attachment to the physical body and its senses, and so it is contained within the body.

This experience is just the result of yang hou (advancing the yang), which is to say that the yang shen (positive vitality) has reached to the *ni wan* cavity, but *is not* an indication of the elixir having been formed. There is no need to attempt duplicating the experience, for to do so will only result in becoming attached to joy (one of the seven p'o spirits) and will eventually bring about fanaticism and mental illness. Let it go, there is much work ahead. Rather, progress by bringing the light into the Golden Court, letting it drop down into the lower tan-tien. When it does so there will be a sound like thunder, then the embryo can be formed. A physical sign that someone has reached this level is when the left eye frequently remains closed. This happens because of an unconscious response to retain the light of the yang shen, preventing its dissipation outward through the eye organ.

The process at this point is what the Taoist calls,

"returning the light to reflect the illumination." For the light must continually be returned to oneself if the elixir is to be obtained. If the light is continually emitted it will exhaust itself. So, the Taoists say, stop the seeing and stop the hearing, return everything to emptiness. Stop the seeing means to continually look inward at the light; stop hearing means to continually listen inwards. Continue until emptiness is achieved, wherein there is no inward and outward. This is returning to the Void.

The sacred sun and sacred moon illuminate the Golden Court. One attainment is eternal attainment.

The "sacred sun" represents the left eye and positive vitality (*yang shen*); the "sacred moon" represents the right eye and negative vitality (*yin shen*). The "Golden Court" is within the brain, usually called the "Third Eye", or in some Taoist texts it is called, *hsuan kuan* (The Mysterious Pass). Actually there are about thirty-six names used in Taoism by various schools to indicate the Golden Court.

This experience is much different than the previous one of wisdom light, as the text now brings us to actual illumination. The difference in one context is that the former is the illumination of the brain organ (the sixth sense organ) and the latter is the illumination of the mind consciousness itself. Not only is the mind sense organ perceived as empty and false, but also the mind consciousness and the sense objects of the mind. This is truly "entering the Void". Once this state is achieved it will remain with you forever, which is why the text adds, *one attainment is eternal attainment.*

In early Taoism, before the Chin and Wei dynasties, the sacred sun and moon were normally referred to as "green dragon, white tiger". These were just references for yang shen and yin shen; the ch'i rising along the left and right sides of the spine respectively. However, it is the harmonizing of these two within the hsuan kuan that brings about true illumination, not their separation, and when they return to the tan-tien together they form the elixir.

In separation the yang shen causes the spirit to leave the body, which is a great experience, but also dangerous. If the spirit does not return quickly it may become attached to such heavenly sights and not return to do the work of forming the immortal foetus. This is the stage referred to in Taoist texts as riding on dragons and/or storks, wandering about the sun or dancing on the moon. The yin shen will also cause the spirit to leave the body, but finds itself in the ghostly and demonic realms. In either case these stages should be foregone so as to continue with the transformational process. The immortal foetus develops only after they have been harmonized and congealed into the elixir within the tan-tien. Once this is accomplished there is further sublimation yet to undergo. Which is, as with the Jade Emperor, to proceed to become a Golden Immortal.

The body will naturally become weightless. When the Supreme Harmony is replete, the bone fragments become like winter jade.

There are numerous stories about Taoist immortals whose bodies were so light that they never left footprints. A Buddhist *lohan* (arhat) is also said to have this same ability so that even insects under his feet will not be killed. But why the body becomes weightless is a very important question. To answer it we must examine why human beings are heavy, or subject to gravity. The first reason, obviously, is our stomach. The Chinese say that the root of human suffering is the stomach. We work to fill it with foods which delight the eye and palate, we even kill other creatures for the sake of our stomachs. The tortoise, a symbol of longevity, lives a long time because it eats very little and does not crave fine delicacies.

To make matters worse the food we put in our stomachs causes many illnesses, even death in some cases. Since the food we ingest sits in our intestines, stomach and bowels many toxins are formed. The Taoists say, "One fart is worth one gold bar to an old man", because poison has left the body. We may or may not wish to accept this but it is thought that cancer is a direct result of eating meat - not that the meat is necessarily rotten, rather that the spirit of the animal seeks its hateful revenge on the person who ate it. This is the karma of "You kill me, I kill you." Another problem is that tension, fear and anxiety usually first strike the stomach and the viscera surrounding it, creating many illnesses and diseases.

In Taoist thought, the p'o (earthly spirit) resides over the physical body, and the nature of p'o is to descend not ascend. Whatever keeps the body heavy and subject to gravity is supported by the p'o. The hun (heavenly spirit) resides over the spiritual body. Its nature is to ascend and not descend, and whatever causes the body to be light and not subject to gravity is supported by the hun. When the Golden Court is illuminated by the sacred sun and moon, the hun then rules over the p'o. The physical body naturally becomes lighter and not subject to gravity.

Another aspect of this is that the new immortal can now begin living off the wind and dew for nourishment, not food and especially not grains and meats which only suffice to make the p'o stronger. For this reason Taoists in their initial training usually subsist on a pure vegetarian diet and/or herbal remedies. Not all Taoist recluses and sects thought this however. Some believed that small amounts of grain and meats periodically kept the body strong and so helped them in the difficult work of cultivation. *Moderation* is the key word here, not abstinence.

The immortal also has permeated his bones with ch'i, thus they become almost pure marrow, much like that of birds or cats. Watch a cat jump and you'll understand how light the bones must be.

When the Supreme Harmony is replete means that when the yin shen and yang shen exist in union within oneself there results the Supreme Harmony, *t'ai ho*, which literally translates as "the highest union". This union of yin shen and yang shen is the elixir of immortality. The elixir is refined more and more, just as steel is refined over and over to improve its quality and grade. Through refinement the elixir becomes evermore "replete".

The bone fragments will become like winter jade. Winter jade is white jade or as Taoists like to think of jade, dragon ching. In both Taoist and Buddhist beliefs this winter jade is called *she-li*, which comes from the Sanskirt term *sarira*. This she-li is considered to be physical evidence of a true immortal or lohan. It is supposedly the transformation of bone into marrow and then into a *vajra* (diamond like or indestructible like) substance. Many sages after their departure from the world were cremated and pieces of these winter jade-like bone fragments are found among the ashes, which are then treasured as holy relics.

Attaining the elixir results in immortality, not attaining it results in its extinction.

This is an obvious statement to exhort the cultivator into remembering the fundamental purpose, acquiring the elixir. If the elixir is not acquired we will undergo a common death, which is the separation of hun and p'o.

The elixir is within yourself, it is not white and not green.

Again the text is reminding the cultivator that the alchemy for attaining the elixir of immortality sits directly inside oneself and there is no point in looking externally for some magic pill. Everything needed is contained within. "Not white, not green" is a reference to physical substances such as cinnabar and gold, mercury and lead, which some alchemists consider the basis for the "pill of immortality".

Lu Szu-hsing writes in his appended verses, "*The elixir is called "green dragon and white tiger", this elixir is the nature of no-nature, emptiness of non-emptiness.*" His point here is that nature and no-nature, emptiness and non-emptiness are just called "green dragon and white tiger." Dragons and tigers, green and white are just images of the elixir. The images are used because the true elixir - nature and no-nature, emptiness and non-emptiness - is imageless. Green dragons and white tigers are just expedient symbols used by the Taoist adept before realizing the true elixir.

Lu also writes, "*The two images of the dragon and tiger are unified through ch'i (breath); chaos blending as One.*" The dragon and tiger are also symbols of yin and yang. When true breath (*i-ch'i*) is achieved in meditation the yin and yang are unified. "Chaos" is a term for the primal conditions of yin and yang, before their separation. To return to this primal condition is the nature of no-nature and emptiness of non-emptiness, *the One.*

Recite and hold ten-thousand times. These are the subtle principles for self-illumination.

Reciting and holding here means that you can repeat the entire text by memory, not just reading it. In our modern society we don't accentuate training the memory, choosing rather to let computers and calculators store our information for us. This is a great loss. Computers and calculators are inventions which originally were designed to imitate the mind, but what they really do is weaken the mind, as the mind is one sense like a muscle and needs exercise. In Taoism, as well as Buddhism, memorization of sacred texts and chants were fundamental practices of self-illumination. Once a text is memorized it becomes part of the cultivator, a sealing in of wisdom, influencing their thoughts and actions so the goal of self-illumination can be reached more expediently, as well as being able to draw from the wisdom instantaneously in the face of obstacles. The idea and practice of "mind-seal" begins with the ability to memorize the tenets and processes for attainment.

However, Lu Szu-hsing warns us that "it is not possible to acquire the eternal through just invocation." Just to recite this scripture, no matter how many times, will be in vain if we do not cultivate and attain the elixir - *emptiness of nonemptiness, nature of no-nature*. Recitation or chanting is a practice of mindfulness and mindfulness is the groundwork for tranquility and purity.

These are the subtle principles of self-illumination. All of the above verses refer to the principles for the attainment of self-illumination. Each verse requires much learning and must be developed through intuitive understanding, for they are subtle and mystical. This intuitive understanding can only come from practice and study. For as the text related earlier, "*the sages awaken through self-cultivation; deep, profound, their practices require great effort.*"

The Three Treasures of Immortality

The following is a translation from Hsien Tao Ching Tso Ching *(The Way of Immortals Meditation Classic), compiled by T'ien Chien. Contained within this work is a chapter on the Three Treasures, taken from the records of the* Lung Men *(Dragon Door) sect of Taoism. The piece is a collection of aphorisms and quotes from various Taoist scriptures and masters. Since I found this work not only complementary to, but helpful in the understanding of the Jade Emperor's Mind Seal Classic, I deemed it best to attach it. It contains an abundance of Taoist terminology, which may or may not be difficult for the reader. However, I decided to let the work to stand on its own, without commentary or footnote, wishing to treat the work more as a reference or source document, than as a scripture.*

Translator

Introduction

Ching, ch'i and *shen* activate the human being. If they are not depleted they will work intrinsically to produce the substances needed to remain youthful. The ancients have stated, "Heaven has three treasures - the *sun, moon* and *stars.* Mankind has three treasures - ching, ch'i and shen."

The ching within the human body is an abstract and subtle substance. There are various, broad definitions of ching which describe the particular chings within the human body, such as the chings of the Five Viscera (*wu tsang*). There are even more specific definitions which describe the chings of the reproductive system.

The *restored ching* is defined as *hsien t'ien* (Before Heaven) and *hou t'ien* (After Heaven). You receive the ching of Before Heaven from your parents. In the *Ling Shu Ching*, chapter on "Meridians and Pulses", it says: "A person's life begins with a ching that is initially intact."

The After Heaven ching comes about during the transformation of birth, which then causes the need to eat and drink. The *Su Wen Ching*, in an attached treatise on meridians and pulses, says: "When you eat food, some of the nutrients enter the bone. The excess nutrients overflow the pulses. When you drink, the nutrients go to the stomach. But the excess liquid causes the ching and ch'i to be in surplus and so dissipation occurs." This describes the After Heaven ching. It is only when the After Heaven and Before Heaven chings assist each other that there can be harmony within the body.

The *ch'i* completes the human body, being the primal substance and function of life itself. Everyone has primal (*yuan*) ch'i, also called "true ch'i". There is the ch'i of the viscera and bowels, ch'i of the meridians, ancestral ch'i, cultivated ch'i, protective ch'i and so on. But the most important ch'i is that of your nature (*hsing ch'i*). In the *Bright Peak Record* it says, "A person's life is totally dependent upon their nature ch'i."

The *shen*, unified with ching and ch'i, becomes a single substance which initiates the activity of life. The *Ling Shu*

Ching (Divine Pivot Classic) states, "Both essences (ching and ch'i) when unified are called shen." In the chapter The Man of Harmony Retreats to the Valley, it also says, "The shen resembles a mountain stream of ching and ch'i." The *Ta Ping Ching* (Great Equalling Classic) says, "Humans have ching and ch'i, which results in their obtaining the shen; if the ching and ch'i disperse this will cause the shen to perish."

The average person considers that they have only one type of active thinking consciousness. Yet, if they could restore the shen within they would perceive that this is perfection and that it is the central substance of human life. This is exactly what the *Ling Shu Ching*, in the chapter on Restoring Ching to Transform the Ch'i, means when it states, "Those who acquire this shen flourish; those who lose this shen perish."

The emphasis of *tao kung* (skills of the Way) lies in the *refinement* of shen, the *penetration* of shen and the *guarding* of shen. These three practices are of the utmost importance.

Many ask how the ching, ch'i and shen relate to one another. The *Su Wen Ching* (Plain Questions Classic) states: "Within the ching the ch'i is produced; within the ch'i the shen is produced." The *Liu Ching* (Classification Classic) states: "Perfecting the ching results in the perfecting of ch'i; the perfecting of ch'i results in the perfecting of shen."

The ancient Taoist masters originally transmitted these principles in their treatises so as to make clear that "the refinement of ching results in the transformation of ch'i; the refinement of ch'i results in the transformation of shen; the refinement of shen results in the return to the Void." The Void here means the spiritual heaven of *no-nothingness*. Additionally, "the accumulation of shen produces ch'i and the accumulation of ch'i produces ching."

From the perspective of tao kung the refinement of ching and the production of ch'i nourishes the shen, which strengthens the body. To the novice this is the most important principle.

CHING

(The First Treasure)

The character for *ching* (essence) has the idiom *mi* (rice) along the left side, which is associated with plant seeds. On the right side is *ching*, or greenness and the easterly direction, which are associations of wood. Plants and wood, like food and drink, can be seen in terms of an inner essence and an outer manifestation. Ching is the human body's treasure.

Plants and wood are born of water, which normally peaks during the interim period of *tzu* (the third watch - 11:00 pm to 1:00 am). Tzu is associated with water and the kidneys; the kidneys are the Water Treasury. Tzu is positioned in the northern direction. Therefore, these are born out of the tzu position.

You must repair the damage food causes to the ching. You must daily repair and nourish each of the seven openings as they become damaged by food.

Those who either diminish their ching or lose the ching

through involuntary emissions damage both the shen and ch'i, and the spirit of vitality becomes unrestorable.

The secretions are transmuted into blood, dwelling in the *Red Palace* (heart); the blood transmutes into ching, dwelling in the *Life Gate* (two kidneys); ching then transmutes into heat, dwelling in the *Ocean of Ch'i* (lower abdomen); the ch'i then relies on this warm energy to transmute itself into shen; and, the shen depends on this energy to transmute itself back to its primal condition, *yuan shen*."

The True Man, Tan Yuan (Tranquil Garden) said: "Within a person's body there is but one original energy. Yet, you must return the illumination like reflected light. Gather this energy, sink it as much as possible and abide by it. After a long time, within the midst of yourself you will discover a greater self."

Pao P'o Tzu said: "The substance is warmed by the breath and the water is acquired, resulting in an embryo. The ch'i can transmute the ching."

Ching is man's original constitution (*yuan ching*); blood (*hua*) is the outer manifestation; movement is the result of ching and stillness the result of ch'i. Ching and ch'i operate as one unit. Blood causes the ching and ch'i to unite and become manifest. In the old days this was called "the flower" (*hua*).

In the *Return to the Source Treatise* (Kuei Yuan Lun) it says, "Plants and wood cultivate their essence (ching) in one year, then reveal their flowers. The fruit of all wood is in the flowers; the female embryo is entirely in the blood."

Ching is able to produce ch'i; ch'i is also able to produce ching. Like water becoming clouds, ching can become ch'i. Like clouds becoming water, ch'i can become ching. During spring and summer, the clouds are full of rain, and are excessive. During autumn and winter, the clouds are light and too sparse. When humans are young and strong the ching and ch'i are full. In old age the ching has been dissipated and the ch'i exhausted. This is a natural principle of heaven, earth, man and all phenomena (the ten-thousand things).

Ch'ien Hsu Tzu (Master Concealing Emptiness) said: "The yin within yang is called ching; the yang within the yin is called ch'i. Both of these are mutually dependent and born of each other."

The skills of *refining ching and transmuting ch'i* are ordinarily divided into three stages, the three gatherings of yang (*san ts'ai yang*). The first type of yang is, "to guard low in the tan-tien"; the second is, "to produce yang" or "to return the one yang"; and the third is, "to gather the yang", which is also called, "to gather the herbs and bring them to the stove."

You cannot *refine ching and transmute ch'i* without using wind and fire. Wind means the breath (ch'i), fire the spirit (shen). When the shen enters the ch'i, stimulate it as you would use a bellows for stoking a furnace. This will naturally result in the ching transmuting to ch'i.

To *refine ching and transmute ch'i* you should practice the "quick fire"; to *refine the ch'i and transmute shen* you should practice the "slow fire".

Quick fire means having the sensation of heat; slow fire means not having the sensation of heat.

The ancients said: "It is not necessary to activate a strong fire, as the stove within yourself is already strong enough." This means, the body does not need be hot, as normal body warmth is enough to create the embryo. This is similar to attaining the state of 'being' and 'non-being', where there is also no requirement for experiencing an auspicious inner light, as the mind is already full of light. There is a secret saying, "to refine the ch'i and transmute the shen, nourish the slow fire and breathe without a coming or going. This will most certainly bring about the perfection of bliss."

Refining ching and transmuting ch'i is the Eye Treasury of Buddhism and the "returning the light to reflect the illumination" of Taoism. Lao Tzu said, "without desire, you can contemplate the subtlety (of your True Nature); with desire you can contemplate the boundaries (of your True Nature)". "To contemplate the subtlety without desire" is the method of abstract stillness (contemplation of turning the seeing and hearing inwards). "To contemplate the boundaries with desire" is the method of entering emptiness (contemplation of the Void).

The root method for "refining ching and transmuting ch'i" however is described in the phrase, "with desire you can contemplate the boundaries". The question of how to contemplate the boundaries defines the differences between the northern sect *Tranquility and Purity School* (Ching Ch'ing Pai), and the southern sect *Grafting Shoots School*

(Tsai Chieh Pai). Each takes a different approach.

If you can gather into *one* all that is in front and back of you, above and below, left and right, you will arrive at a state of spiritual void and fixed tranquility. The work of refining ching and transmuting ch'i will then be concluded.

The ching of formlessness is called primal essence (*yuan ching*). When it separates out from its nebulous origin, it is called "turbid ching". Primal ching resides within the primal ch'i and primal shen. This flowery essence begins to form within them, like an invisible treasury within the body.

Tung Hsuan Tzu (Master Universal Mystery) said: "Cultivate the Tao, otherwise you can never come to know the true nature of man and life itself. To pluck the petals in search of the branches is to force the issue. To see flowers sprout in the void has no real validity. It will be most difficult to develop the fruit if you lose the nutrition of the primal essence (yuan ching)."

Ch'ien Hsu Tzu said: "To obstruct the shen results in congestion of the ching. If the ching is congested the result is dissipated ch'i; dissipated ch'i results in the obstruction of forming the elixir."

Ts'an T'ung (Penetrating Equality) said: "It is very difficult to perceive the subtlety of primal essence (yuan ching) and to understand the subtle convergence it undergoes in forming the elixir."

The primal essence (yuan ching) is without substance and so is difficult to observe; turbid essence does have substance and is quite evident.

When primal ching begins to move, let it take its own course. Even during the transmuting process it still has the substance of turbid ching. The substance is important, even though it is the lowest grade of ching.

The Way of the immortals, in the end, lies in the refinement of the ching and transmutation of ch'i. Ch'i is light and floats upwards. When this occurs all outflows (desires and emissions) of ching will naturally cease.

Li Tao Chun (Plum of Pure Tao) said: "First refine the ching, then use the ch'i to refine it further. When refining, always be aware of the sensations of ching ascending."

Without this Taoist discipline of smelting, the ching is nothing more than the turbid ching of After Heaven; smelting the ching creates the primal essence of the Before Heaven. Without this discipline, the ch'i is just the ordinary breath of the After Heaven; with this discipline it becomes the primal vitality (yuan ch'i) of Before Heaven. Without this discipline, the spirit is just the knowledge of After Heaven spirit; with this discipline it becomes the primal spirit (yuan shen) of Before Heaven spirit.

If the methods of the After Heaven seem too vague and difficult, and you are unable to perceive the workings of the Before Heaven do nothing else other than continue with the practice and refinement of the After Heaven methods until such time that the workings of the Before Heaven become do clear.

CH'I

(The Second Treasure)

Purity is heavenly (*t'ien*) ch'i; impurity is earthly (*ti*) ch'i.

Motion is yang ch'i; stillness is yin ch'i.

Heaven's purity is pure yang; earth's impurity is pure yin.

The movement of heaven lies in the circularity of *ch'ien*; earth's stillness lies in the squareness of *k'un*.

With regard to heaven, *purity, impurity, movement* and *stillness* are projections through which the sun and moon appear.

With regard to earth, they are projections through which the seasons appear.

With regard to mankind, they are projections through which the wise and average appear. The sage is yang and through the casting off of his mortal shell becomes an ascending immortal. The average person is yin and dies in old age to become a spirit or ghost.

When true ch'i is spread throughout the viscera it becomes visceral ch'i, such as: heart ch'i, lung ch'i, spleen ch'i, stomach ch'i, liver ch'i and kidney ch'i. So to begin with you must strengthen and nourish *the ch'i of the five viscera*.

When true ch'i flows throughout the meridian routes it becomes *the ch'i of the meridian routes*. When the ch'i is fully gathered it will proceed to become meridian ch'i.

Regulated ch'i works together with the blood to stimulate the ch'i within the pulses and arteries.

Protective ch'i is the ch'i which gives motion to those things external to the pulses and arteries (the flesh and bones). However, if your temperament is either fearful, cruel or deceitful the ch'i will be obstructed in the pulses and meridians, as well as in those parts which are external to the pulses and arteries.

Ancestral ch'i is the ch'i which has accumulated within the heart/mind. True ch'i comes from *ching ch'i* (essence and vitality) contained within the kidneys, which is to say the ch'i that is inherited from your parents. When the ch'i reaches the *shui ku* ("water valley" - stomach), it alters the stomach and spleen's metabolism of life-giving foods.

In relation to the lungs, there are three divisions in which the breath is drawn in. These must be combined together in order to be complete. There is an *active* and lively type of ch'i which is very powerful, yet in substance, abstract. There is a *flowing* ch'i which penetrates throughout the entire body without any hindrance. There is *mobilized* ch'i. The storehouse of yang is within the yin, just as fire is concealed within water. Obtaining this ch'i is a matter of before heaven. Your longevity will depend on your degree of this ch'i.

Movement results in the manifestation of ching; tran-

quility results in the manifestation of ch'i. The ch'i mobilizes
the breath and blood within the body. Then the ears can
hear, the eyes can see, the hands can grasp, and the feet can
walk. Each of these are the result of ch'i force. The very
essence of a person's life is also a result of ch'i, as well as
birth itself.

That which is named "strong" is called "life".

The storehouse is regarded as *k'an* (water).

True ch'i (breath) lies within emptiness, which is the
breath of neither inhaling nor exhaling. Likewise, the ch'i of
the True One is Before Heaven.

The Yellow Court Classic (Huang Ting Ching) says:
"Immortality is conferred through inhalation and exhalation
of primal ch'i".

Ts'ui Hsu Yin (Reciter of the Pure Void) said: "Ch'i is
not merely ch'i - as breath, but rather the very vapour of the
original substance."

Before Heaven ch'i is acquired through the two ch'i's of
the mother and father at the time of their intercourse. Their
union attracts you and in the midst of their intercourse you
attach yourself to them.

After Heaven ch'i comes about at the time you leave the
womb and with a loud shout become a prisoner of the earth.
At this time the ch'i enters the nose and mouth.

Before Heaven ch'i is just like the roots of a tree, seeking the source, of water. After Heaven ch'i is just like the leaves of the tree which rely on the circulation of water. Therefore, if the Before Heaven ch'i is exhausted, the After Heaven ch'i will be severed. Similarly, if the tree's roots are severed, the leaves will wither, and if the source of the water is wanting then the circulation will cease. Before Heaven ch'i and After Heaven ch'i cannot become deficient if they are stabilized and regulated in an orderly fashion.

Novices ask, "What is called "Before and After Heaven?" Regulated respiration through the nose and

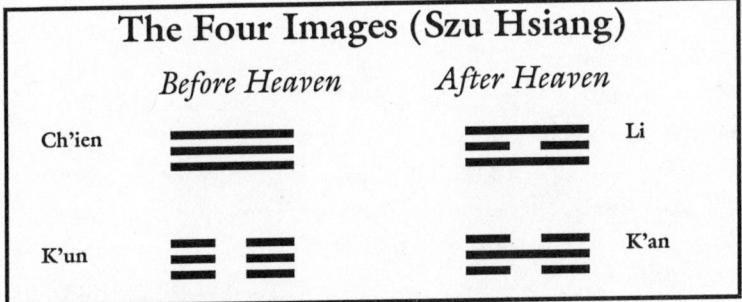

mouth are After Heaven. Unregulated respiration brings about death and is Before Heaven. *K'an* and *Li* are After Heaven; *Ch'ien* and *K'un* are Before Heaven.

Another question is, "How much time will it take to acquire the Before Heaven ch'i? The answer is that when the shen is pure you can recapture your youth and witness the wonderful results of your efforts. You will retain this state even when relaxing at your leisure. You can achieve the Before Heaven in one hundred days of internal cultivation.

The source of Tao is not external to shen and ch'i; shen and ch'i unite as one.

The complete repair of the ch'ien (heaven) within the body is a result of transmuting ching, transmuting the shen and then "returning to the Void". You advance with every step.

Silence protects the ch'i; "entering purity and leaving the turbid," restores the ch'i; "swallowing from above and quivering below" gathers the ch'i; continuous preservation harmonizes the ch'i; through following natural tendencies you will circulate the ch'i.

Preserve your imagination so that you can exhibit the ch'i in any manner. The Tao Yin (breath control methods) attacks illnesses by mobilizing ch'i. The Taoist naturally nourishes the ch'i and so can achieve long-life. The Confucian nourishes the ch'i of magnanimity, concerned only for the quality of life and death. These are like past and present men who with great determination and benevolence, would give up their life in the sight of danger or sacrifice their life to preserve their integrity.

So when nourishing the ch'i be pure of mind, let moral principles nourish the ch'i. Fill the entire universe, and achieve greatness; attain an indestructibility that can never be extinguished.

Because shen and ch'i are one whole, they are forever contained within the space between heaven and earth.

What is it to refine ch'i and transmute shen? This is *k'an* (water) and *li* (fire) uniting within the body; the advancing and withdrawing of heaven (ch'ien).

There is water within ch'i, in the form of a buoyant mist, yet it does not easily ascend. If not refined the water dissipates and scatters. You must transmute this water and allow it to sink downward. The way of immortals calls this "disciplining the true fire." If the water dissipates it will leave entirely and the ch'i will be completely exhausted. Awareness that the ch'i has been transmuted will in turn stimulate the shen.

The analogy "clouds and mists" relates to a sudden illumination of *t'ai yang* (like sunlight bursting forth through the clouds). A burning flame is produced from the water within the ch'i (like lightning and thunder from rain clouds). The water then disperses. When the clouds and mists disappear the yang illumination is complete.

Chang Tzu-yang (Eternal, Purple-yang) said: "The Heavenly Man (immortal) is originally identical with true ch'i. The existence of his physical body causes no further spiritual obstructions. His refinement penetrates both form and the unseen (yin fu) aspects of shen, creating a totally harmonious condition. He is therefore aware that form and substance are but True Void."

Employing the shen to regulate the ch'i results from heating the ching, which nourishes its original harmonious condition, at which point the ch'i will circulate without cease. This is the attainment of perfect conditions, as it is with steam when it condenses into a liquid state. You will then be able to unite the shen with the body, producing long-life, youthfulness and fulfillment of your destiny and nature. From below (the earthly) you now take ascent (to the heavenly).

Ts'ui Tu Tzu (Master Azure Void) said: "The most important aspect of the elixir is that of Before Heaven ch'i. Then the work of refinement is like turning a yellow stalk into a jade flower."

Yuan Tu Tzu (Master Within Causation) said: "The ch'i neither dwells in a place above or below man's body, nor does it dwell within the body; it is neither internal or external; it is formless and imageless."

San-feng Tsu (Ancestor Three Peaks) said: "True Before Heaven ch'i is acquired through gathering. Then just proceed slowly with cooking and simmering over the fire."

Chin Kao (Gold Conferrer) said: "True Before Heaven ch'i is a mark of the void; circulation of true ch'i creates marrow, not dried wood."

Yu Yang Tzu (Master Jade Yang) said: "True Before Heaven ch'i at its source, is formlessness, but amazingly it can bring to life that which has form."

Tzu Yang Tsu (Ancestor Purple Yang) said: "True Before Heaven ch'i is a mark of true lead. Do not believe in false teachings designed to deceive disciples of the Way for profit."

Chung Tsu (Ancestor Goblet) said: "Intelligent men obtain Before Heaven ch'i through gathering, then in one night the thunder is heard and they no longer rest for even a minute until the elixir is complete."

Chung Yang Tsu (Ancestor Double Yang) said: "Inhaling and exhaling are mutually responsive. When the pulses move the breath rests. Abstraction is produced through tranquility; within the greatness of abstraction is Before Heaven ch'i, coming forth from within the void."

SHEN

(The Third Treasure)

Shen (spirit) dwells within each person. It gives life and mental activity to each of us. The broad definition of shen is *ching shen* (essence and spirit), or the spirit of vitality. The specific definition is the brightness of the eyes, for the eyes act as the home and focus of the shen.

Shen represents fire (*li*); ch'i represents water (*k'an*). After Heaven ch'i and shen are visible in the forms of fire and water.

Concealed within water is perfect tranquility. Within the kidneys the ching transmutes into ch'i.

Concealed within fire is perfect movement. Within the mind is shen. Shen causes the fire to ascend.

Before Heaven shen is like fire within wood and stone; within the eyes shen is like a burning beacon, even if you are unable to see it. This is the primal shen.

Between heaven and earth dwells fire and water. Between the eyes the illumination causes the ch'i to rise. Is this not the same as the sound of thunder produced by clouds and rain between heaven and earth?

Heaven and earth, sun and moon, are all able to exist for a long time. Man's body employs fire and water and is then subject to decay. However, if man imitates the ways of heaven and earth, sun and moon, this condition can be reversed and we can exist as long as heaven and earth, the sun and moon.

Ling Pao Tu Jen Ching (Classic on Saving Men with the Treasures of the Immortals) says: "When the shen and ch'i unite in the subtlety of the Great Void, there is no life and death. Entering formlessness is establishing the Tao. Therefore, employ the workings of fire and water within yourself. When the shen ascends fire and water are needed no more."

There is fire within shen, just as there is fire within wood. Though not perceptible this does not detract from the truth of its potentiality. So it is with the shen within yourself. The *Ta Tao Ko* (Song of the Great Tao) says: "Circulate the breath, for within it is true breath. Refine the shen, for within it is true shen. Perceptible breath is not true breath; the perceptible mind is not true shen. The immortal discovers the true breath and true shen. Average men only know inhalation and exhalation, and the rational mind. This is why the immortals talk of primal ch'i and primal shen."

Primal shen is beyond thought and beyond imagination. It reveals itself only through tranquility and ultimate emptiness, where in one instant you are awakened to the experience of primal shen. Knowing this you will understand thoroughly the meaning of producing heaven, earth and the ten-thousand things."

Ch'ien Hsu Tsu (Ancestor Hidden Within Emptiness) said: "Primal shen acts as your nature. It is the master of ching and ch'i. When the primal shen unites with these two its potential cannot be fathomed, for then the process of attaining immortality is methodless. This is called the natural workings of shen. So just cultivate your nature and skills. The shen will then perfect itself."

Ancestor Lu (Tung-pin) described four steps in which immortality is attained. This is truly the method of no method:

Forgetting yourself entirely nourishes the ch'i. You then attain the medicines.

Forgetting entirely about the ch'i fixes the shen. The elixir is then congealed.

Forgetting entirely about the shen is returning to the Void.

Forgetting entirely about the Void is uniting with the Tao. In emptiness the elixir is complete.

The only ingredients needed are purity of heart and tranquility of mind, where returning to the Void will be a natural process.

The Chinese Phonetic Text, for Recitation

For those with a feeling and inclination for the ritual aspects of self-cultivation, the following phonetic text for recitation is provided. The English version may also be used by those not versed in Chinese. Either version will do.

The proper manner of performing the ritual is to place a likeness of the Jade Emperor or Three Pure Ones in or above the center and back of a shrine table. Place lit candles and flowers to each side of an incense burner. In front of the incense burner place three small cups, offering tea, cooked rice and fruit or vegetables in each of these respectively. Make sure the area you recite in is quiet and clean. Place three lit pieces of incense in the burner. Bow three times, touching your head to the floor, and recite each time "Praise to the Heavenly Ruler, the Jade Emperor, Highest Sovereign of Heaven and all immortals". When your head is touching the floor during each bow mentally offer the flowers, candles, tea, rice, vegetables and incense to the Jade Emperor, visualizing yourself as before him in his heavenly palace. Offer these things in hopes of receiving an auspicious response to the recitation of his scripture. During the entire ritual keep a reverent and quiet mind. When done reciting bow three more times as before. Finally, light three more pieces of incense and place them outdoors in either a burner or in the ground. Bow three times at the conclusion of each recitation.

Yuh Hwang Shin Yinn Jing
(repeat above line three times)
Shang yaw san piin
Shern yeu chee jing
Huaang huaang hu hu
Yeau yeau ming ming
Tsurn wuu shoou yoou
Ching keh erl cherng
Jeong feng heunn her
Bae ryh gong ling
Moh chaur shang dih
Yi jih fei sheng
Jy jee yih wuh
Mey jee nan shyng
Lyuu jiann tian guang
Hu shi yuh ching
Chu shyuan ruh piin
Rouh wang rouh tsurn
Mian mian buh jyue
Guh dih shen gen
Rern geh yeoh jing
Jing her chyi shern
Shern yeu chee her
Chee her tii jen
Buh der chyi jen
Jie shyh chiaang ming
Shern neng ruh shyr

Shern neng fei shyng
Ruh shwei buh nih
Ruh huoo buh fern
Shern yi shyng sheng
Jing yi chee yng
Buh diau buh tsarn
Song bor ching ching
San piin yi lii
Miaw buh keh ting
Chyi jiuh tzer yeoh
Chyi sann tzer ling
Chi chiaw shiang tong
Chiaw chiaw guang ming
sheng ryh sheng yeoh
jaw yaw jin tyng
Yi der yeong der
Tsyh ran shen ching
Taih her chung yih
Guu sahn harn chyong
Der dan tzer ling
Dan tsay shen jong
Buh der tzer ching
Dan tzay shen jong
Fay bor fei ching
Song chyr wann biann
Miaw lii tsyh ming

Translator's Afterword

I realize how difficult it is sometimes to wade through the cryptic and abstruse passages of Taoist manuals such as this, in order to find "the method". What follows is a gleaning of personal insights, based on my own experience of these processes. My words are brief. Words are limited in depth and this subject is unlimited in depth. Much however can be gained by both study and practice. As Master Liang advised me, "never discourage the critical need for a student to both study and practice." Hopefully I can in some small measure, make the task of meditation a bit more understandable and practical for the beginner.

For the beginner the best method of meditation is counting the breaths. This consists only of concentrating on the tan-tien and counting mentally on each exhalation. When reaching the count of ten exhalations, start over and count to ten exhalations again, and just continue this. When able to do this proficiently, begin mentally acknowledging each exhalation, not the inhalation.

After a period of time the methods may be dropped and you will be able to sit and just focus on the tan-tien without thoughts of counting or exhalations. Whenever you have difficulty concentrating simply direct both eyes to the tip of the nose with the eyes slightly open, this will help you concentrate more steadily.

It is suggested that to enhance your meditation practice you also employ the practice of *Pa Tuan Chin* (Eight Pieces of Brocade). This is an internal seated yoga set of Taoist exercises which can provide very helpful benefits to your meditation practice.

When sitting (meditating), just sit. Don't hold judgements about good sitting or bad sitting, just sit. If your schedule only allows you to sit a few minutes each day, then sit those few minutes each day and if possible make that time the same each day. Repetitious practice is the true key to success. The art of sitting relies on three basics:

Constantly be mindful of your posture and adjust the part of the body which feels awkward.

Focus all your attention on the tan-tien in the lower abdomen, not on the breath (unless using the counting method).

When thoughts arise, let them go and return to focusing on the tan-tien.

In time sitting becomes a very natural and comfortable experience. Before that happens however there are two states of mind which cause most people to stop their practice. The first is *distraction*; thoughts arise and lead you far away from your focusing. The second is *obscurity;* this is sleepiness, dullness and exhaustion. Only time, patience and forbearance can cure these problems. Every day just sit and eventually these obstacles disappear.

Never attempt to make the breath slow, deep and long. Let this happen of its own accord. The breath will settle if you allow it to. Once it is settled you will experience what is called "true breath", which means that your mind-intent (or will) controls it, not your thoughts. At this point you will not be aware of the breath, much like a baby who just naturally breathes.

Within the stage of restoring or refining ching, do not resort to the sexual techniques described in various Taoist manuals. Ching is restored and refined not by exercises and techniques, but by mind. These can be dangerous psychologically and physically, as some techniques are very powerful. If the mind isn't ready to deal with it, then the results tend towards the negative.

The very essence of restoring ching lies in only two things:

Moderation in emission and purifying the mind of sexual excesses.

Moderation in eating and purifying the mind of bad eating habits.

If these can be accomplished and linked with daily sitting, the gathered ch'i will in the end refine the ching, and it is through the positive effects of sitting that the mind is gradually purified of such things. Like the breath, it will occur naturally over time. Neither purity nor tranquility can be forced into the mind, otherwise you will have the same result as an ant trying to eat a watermelon in one bite.

Taoism never espoused the idea that sexual techniques or celibacy, vegetarianism or fasting, should be forced into a life style, rather that tranquility of itself cured sexual excesses and unwanted emission, gluttony and bad habits. They rely on pure mind to naturally eradicate these things from our nature. This is like Buddha's analogy from the *Surangama Sutra* of letting the debris in a glass of water settle by not agitating the water. Our mind and body are no different. Gradually you will reach a state called, "no outflows". Then the energy we normally put into inappropriate expressions of sex, conduct and eating is not expressed externally and thereby dissipated. Instead the energy is returned and retained internally to do the work of refinement. If you really want to understand how much energy is expended externally, try not speaking for one month. Words cannot describe how vital you become internally from doing this.

If you continue your practice you will eventually be able to turn your hearing and sight inwards. This stage is called "Accumulating Light." Nothing external can disturb your tranquility, even when not sitting. When you close your eyes and look inward there will be light; turning your hearing inward there will be perfect silence. There will also be one or all of the following three experiences, not always when sitting, and not in any specific order. They can occur in any relaxed situation and can be either intense or mild. The following is just a generalized description, it is not meant to be an emphatic guide, just a rule of thumb.

First you will internally see what appears to be a thousand tiny lamps lighting up the entire inside of the top of your head; *secondly*, there will be a flash of bright white light followed immediately by a loud thunderous sound in the ears and in some cases a profound sense of lightness of the body; *thirdly*, there will be an all-encompassing soft, white and cloud like light, along with a warmth generated in the lower abdomen. The first experience is accompanied by an incredible sense of joy; the second, a sense of absolute cleanliness; the third, perfect ease. None of these should be attached to. Just continue sitting and letting go of the sensations. Otherwise you'll just stagnate and not progress.

Depending on the Before Heaven ch'i (inherited ch'i), some will experience these states, in part or in whole, with very little practice. For some it takes longer as they need to further develop their After Heaven ch'i (cultivated ch'i). There is no guarantee that everyone will experience the same thing. Each of us are different and therefore you may or may not have these experiences in the exact manner described.

Before these experiences occur they are usually preceded by either horrifying dream states, migraine type headaches, a sense of uneasiness, paranoia or an intense desire for sex or eating. These pass relatively quickly if you are aware of them and thus are not a real concern. They are just the negative aspects (p'o) reacting to the awakening of hun, just like a flaring up of a candle before it goes out.

There is also the problem, in reverse of the above, wherein the dream states are incredibly enjoyable, like visiting heavenly realms; giddiness in your daily activities, seeing raindrop-like images floating about in the air or hearing mumbled voices off in the distance. Again, let them go and they will pass quickly. These are just the yang aspects (hun) releasing themselves from the bonds of yin (p'o). More simply, your spiritual nature is waking up and breaking out of its shell. The more proficient you become at meditation the less you will dream. This is the result of an increased state of tranquility.

The real problem for anyone who undertakes the practice of meditation is patience. We want results quickly and the aforementioned obstacles usually cause dismay. So we halt our practice. Many also have difficulty in understanding the concept of emptiness and why it is the goal of meditation. Lu Szu-hsing quotes in his appended verses, *"The term emptiness embraces the entire teaching."* Emptiness is not empty, it is full of light. If we don't empty ourselves, light cannot enter. The obstacles of distraction and obscurity block the light of our true nature. In our Western society many psychologists have expressed their fears about the idea of emptiness or no-thought. Their mistake (and lack of experience) in this matter has been the inability to understand that it is not thought which is cut off, for the very nature of non-thinking requires thought. It is not thought which is cut off, rather the attachment to thought; the six senses are not cut off, the attachment to them is; emptiness is achieved through non-attachment to thought and sense data. There is an enormous difference between the ideas of "no-thought" (extremist view) and "non-attachment to thought."

If you can just steadfastly sit, illumination will occur. There really is no secret other than patience. Our minds are no different than the clouds and rain. If we are patient they will pass and the bright sun will shine. The deep blue skies are then filled with light. This sky is like the empty mind and the shen is the light.

The real work now begins with "returning the light and reflecting the illumination", which is the work of mindfulness, of just sitting and turning the sight and hearing inwards, until a thunderous type of noise is heard coming from deep within the lower abdomen. Continue your practice, just sitting, without backsliding until . . .

Unfortunately my knowledge and experiences do not go beyond this, so I dare not make the pretense of more accomplished states, lest the immortals look down in dismay and report me to the Jade Emperor with the accusation of false speech and the god Erh Lang is sent to arrest me. What I dare add is to just keep sitting until the elixir is formed and let your spirit embryo grow, which is the advice left to us by all immortals and sages, calling it "patient endurance". Avoid being like the farmer in the Sung dynasty who couldn't wait for his crops to grow and so went into his fields at night and pulled all the shoots upwards, only to find his entire crop withered and dead in the morning.

About the Translator

Stuart Alve Olson began learning the Chinese language, along with Buddhist and Taoist philosophy, during his residency at the City of Ten-Thousand Buddhas in Ukiah, California (1979-1980). In 1982 he was invited to live in Master Liang's home in St. Cloud, Minnesota (the only student granted this honor). Staying with Master Liang for five years, Stuart studied both T'ai Chi Ch'uan, Chinese language and philosophy under his tutelage. Since that time he has travelled extensively throughout the United States with Master Liang assisting him in teaching T'ai Chi Ch'uan. Stuart has also taught in Canada, Indonesia and travelled throughout Asia. He lives in Minneapolis, Minnesota where he teaches T'ai Chi Ch'uan, meditation and related Chinese disciplines at the Institute of Internal Arts. He compiles and translates various Taoist, Buddhist and T'ai Chi Ch'uan oriented books for Dragon Door Publications.

About the Cover Artwork and Frontispiece

Ch'ing dynasty, early nineteenth century, Taoist priest robe. Embroidered satin. The central figure in the robe is the Jade Emperor, surrounded by his court, imperial dragons and phoenixes. Cranes, symbols of longevity, border the sleeves. The hem contains the Eight Immortals along with their associated images of the *Pa Kua* (Eight Diagrams).

More Titles
from
Dragon Door Publications

Cultivating the Ch'i
Chen Kung Series, Volume One

Translated by Stuart Alve Olson
$12.95, paper, 164 pages,
5-1/2" x 8-1/2",
101 illustrations.
ISBN 0-938045-11-3

Your foundation for health and self-defense, this is the first English translation of a work considered by the Chinese to be the Bible of T'ai Chi Ch'uan.

Taken from the training notes of T'ai Chi's most famous family, the Yangs, the book gives you detailed advice on breathing techniques, energy generation, meditation, ch'i-kung and much more.

You will appreciate the insightful commentary by Stuart Olson, based on his own extensive experience as a T'ai Chi instructor.

"Chen Kung's book is without question second to none on the subject of T'ai Chi Ch'uan." — *Master T.T. Liang*

"If you are interested in physical immortality, practice yoga, meditate or would like to explore a very ancient, revered and effective way of maintaining physical vitality and youthfulness, you can learn a lot from this book that you would simply never find elsewhere."
— *New Age Retailer*

Imagination Becomes Reality
The Teachings of Master T.T. Liang

Compiled by Stuart Alve Olson
$19.95, paper, 292 pages,
7" x 11", 600 illustrations.
ISBN 0-938045-09-1

T.T. Liang is one of the most revered living masters of T'ai Chi Ch'uan. Now in his nineties, he has taught T'ai Chi for over fifty years. As a senior student to Cheng Man-ch'ing and as author of the best-selling *T'ai Chi Ch'uan for Health and Self-Defense* he helped introduce T'ai Chi to America.

This book presents the very heart of Liang's teachings, including his own version of the Yang style 150 posture solo form. Taken from T.T.'s own notes, this is the most comprehensive description of the form ever presented. Rare interviews and articles by T.T. Liang explore the basic principles and meaning of this increasingly popular martial art.

The remarkable photography both captures the full power, grace and subtlety of T'ai Chi while providing a detailed count by count presentation of each posture.

"*Master T.T. Liang is a Chinese martial arts treasure in Western society. He was a true pioneer in the development of T'ai Chi Ch'uan in the United States of America.*"
— Dr. Yang Jwing-ming,
author of *Yang Style T'ai Chi Ch'uan*

"*This profound yet practical book...has much to offer practitioners of T'ai Chi and those intrigued by the concept of heightened awareness.*"
—Australian Bookseller and Publisher

Order Form

Name _____ Phone_____

Address _____

City _____ State_____ ZIP_____

Country _____

Title	Price	Quantity	Total Price
Cultivating the Ch'i	$12.95	_____	_____
Imagination Becomes Reality	$19.95	_____	_____
Jade Emperor	$10.95	_____	_____

Subtotal _____

MN Residents add
6.5% Sales Tax _____

Shipping & Handling ($2.00 for first
book, $0.75 for each additional book.
Double S&H for non-U.S. orders.) _____

Total _____

❏ Check/Money Order Enclosed
❏ VISA   ❏ Mastercard   Expires _____

Card # _____

Signature _____

Credit Card orders only: 1-800-247-6553

Dragon Door Publications

P.O. Box 4381, St. Paul, MN 55104

ph. (612)645-0517

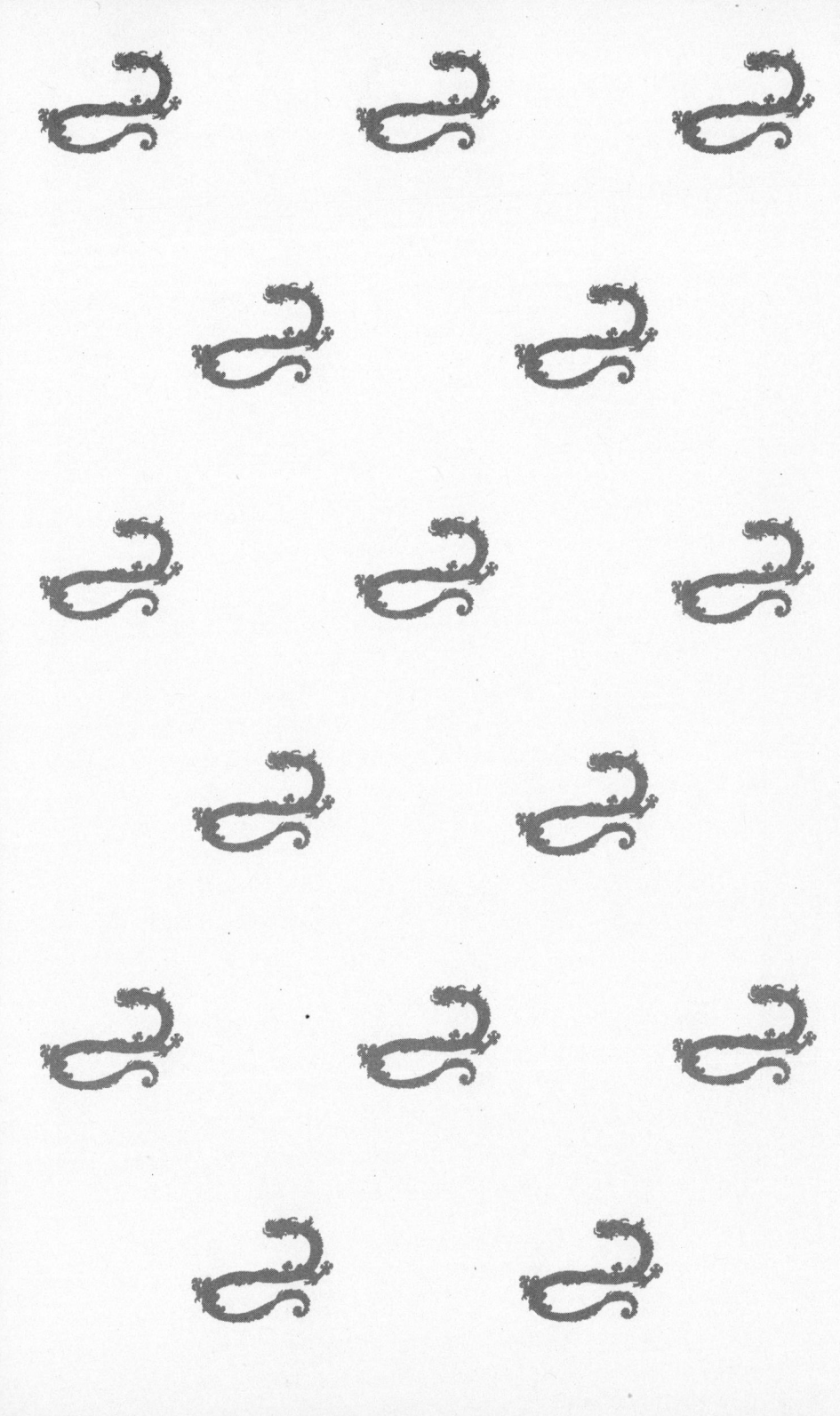